WINNING WEB SITES

Plan and design your own

Bob Whitcroft

Self-Counsel Press
(a division of)
International Self-Counsel Press Ltd.

Printed in Canada

First edition: November 1997

Canadian Cataloguing in Publication Data

Whitcroft, Bob, 1951-
Winning web sites

(Self-counsel series)
ISBN 1-55180-123-X

1. Business enterprises — Computer networks. 2. Web sites — Design. 3. World Wide Web (Information retrieval system) I. Title. II. Series.
TK5105.888.W54 1997   658.054674   C97-910598-6

Self-Counsel Press
(a division of)
International Self-Counsel Press Ltd.

1704 N. State Street   1481 Charlotte Road
Bellingham, WA 98225   North Vancouver, B.C. V7J 1H1
U.S.A.   Canada

*Thanks to everyone involved in Fleet House
for their unfailing commitment to our company,
our customers, and our services.*

Contents

SAMPLES

TABLES

WORKSHEETS AND BLANK FORMS

FIGURES

INTRODUCTION

The Internet, and its World Wide Web component, has matured to the extent that it now makes good business sense to include a Web site in your overall marketing plan.

Regardless of the size of your business, the decision to create a Web site is an exciting one. It is an opportunity for you to create an extremely powerful communications vehicle capable of delivering your company's message around the globe. It is important to remember that the Web site you will create is less about technology than it is about message, content, and image.

Producing the highest quality site requires that you have direct input into the site planning and design processes. This book gives you the benefit and advantage of years of Web site planning, design, production, and hosting experience.

Winning Web Sites will help anyone design a professional, effective Web site quickly and easily while avoiding many of the pitfalls people often experience as they develop their first Web site.

The book will move you quickly through the planning processes that are used by industry experts to achieve winning Web sites for all sorts of businesses. Following these processes will result in a blueprint for a Web site that meets the unique needs of your business.

The time required to complete the planning process will vary from business to business, depending on factors such as:

- Size and sophistication of the site
- Size of your organization
- Size and availability of the project team
- Approval process
- Availability of existing content
- Commitment to the project and its timetable

Most small- to medium-sized companies can easily complete the Web site planning process within a few days. Many companies have complete Web sites operational in this time. Larger companies may require more time to complete the process.

Winning Web Sites is designed to take you through the planning and design processes comfortably, with a clear overview of the later stages of Web site development. You should read through this book once before starting to plan your Web site. The entire process will make more sense when you understand the component parts.

Winning Web Sites guides you through a two-stage process. In the first stage, you will review the scope of the design process. In chapter 1, you will define your site's objectives and focus, using the Site Preplanner. You will also make important decisions such as setting the date by which your site must be launched, as well as determining who will maintain and promote the site. Chapter 2 discusses your Web site production options, so you can begin thinking about how you will produce the site — in-house, using your own skills and those of your staff, or externally, using a production service. Chapter 3 analyzes the cost of both planning and producing your Web site, while chapter 4 discusses the process- and content-planning stage.

In the second stage, you will begin the actual design process. Chapter 5 will introduce you to typical Web site layouts, giving you a brief overview of three common types of Web sites. Chapter 6 then leads you into the actual design, as you begin to design the infrastructure of your site by filling in your own Web Site Planning Map. In chapter 7, you will assemble the individual Web pages of your site — the pages you have mapped out in the previous chapter. Once you have completed these page-planning worksheets, you will do a review of your design in chapter 8. Chapters 9 and 10 discuss promotion and maintenance of your site — both important elements of a Web site.

A *Winning Web Sites* on-line help desk, which will answer many of your frequently asked questions, is available on the Web at *www.sitestowin.com*.

Depending on your experience level and timetable, you may wish to spend more time on some sections and less on others. If you need to use the "express lane," feel free to skip directly to the planning stage beginning in chapter 6, referring to the preceding chapters as necessary rather than reading through the entire book before you begin.

Once you have finished working through the worksheets, you have two options: create your Web site in-house or hire an external production team. Both options are discussed in more detail in chapter 2. If you choose to use an external production service, you may wish to consider using Fleet House, which offers a low-cost, easy-to-use Web site production package and will reimburse you for the cost of this book if you use its services. Details are at the back of the book in Appendix 3. You're now set to begin the process.

1 GETTING STARTED: THE SITE PREPLANNER

At the beginning of the Web site design process, you will have many questions. Some of these questions, and many others, are listed on Worksheet #1, the Site Preplanner. As you start answering the questions in this document (located in Appendix 1), you will begin creating a general plan for your Web site. This process will clarify the goal of your business's Web site and set you on the most efficient course to developing a Web site that meets those goals. Whether you have a team of staff people working on the site or you are the "chief cook and bottle-washer," this stage should bring the necessary elements together in the least possible time.

Start filling in the Site Preplanner after reading the upcoming section of explanatory text. If you can't answer all the questions at this stage, don't worry. The Site Preplanner should be considered a living document, something that changes and grows as your needs become more defined. You can put the information that you know right now into the Site Preplanner, then come back to change, modify, and expand the rest of it as your Web site concept becomes more concrete. Sample #1 shows how one company filled in a Site Preplanner.

a. YOUR SITE'S FOCUS

The first thing you need to determine is the focus of your Web site. How do you expect this focus to change over the next 12 months and further into the future? Most sites are designed with a clear focus on either the organization, its products, or a specific event or promotion. Most sites have a similar structure but differ in content, size, and application.

TIP:

It will likely take a while for you to determine the site objective and message. This is as it should be, as these are the foundations of the Web site project. Take the time to think, discuss, review, and document these two issues.

What will this site be focused on, and how is this focus expected to change in the future?

❏ Our organization   ☒ Our product(s)   ❏ An event or specific promotion

Detail: <u>Present detailed information about Pearlsea products</u>
<u>emphazizing quality, consistency and dependability. Provide</u>
<u>information of interest such as how to prepare product, storage</u>
<u>etc.</u>

What is our primary objective in creating this site?

☒ Promotion   ❏ Generating sales   ❏ Education service/support

Detail: <u>Promotion of Pearlsea products is the priority, focus on</u>
<u>quality and product information within the site.</u>

What message should the site deliver and who is the audience? <u>Our products are</u>
<u>of the highest quality. The oyster that we produce is clean,</u>
<u>nutritious and delicious. Pearlsea is a source of consistent high</u>
<u>quality products all year long and is geared to serve commercial</u>
<u>clients.</u>

Are there existing messages and/or established images that must be incorporated in the Web site? <u>Pearlsea has established logos and product identities.</u>

Detail: <u>The Pearlsea site should utilize and conform to existing</u>
<u>company and product logos, Pearlsea, Pearl Bay and Summer Ice</u>
<u>logos are to be used.</u>

Is there a critical launch date?   ❏ Yes   ☒ No

Detail: <u>There is no set launch date, however it is hoped that this</u>
<u>process may be completed within 30 days.</u>

SAMPLE #1 — Continued

What is the anticipated/required launch date? <u>June 1, 199-</u>

How will we define and quantify success or failure?

Success: <u>Success will be achieved if our Web site generates visibility and new sales over the first year exceeding the production and operating costs of the site. We expect to easily achieve this.</u>

Failure: <u>The site will be seen as a failure if it does not attract interest from the base of prospective customers and if insufficient incremental sales are generated to pay for the site.</u>

Who will have responsibility for maintaining the site? <u>Our owner/manager</u>

Determine what you need to communicate to your target audience to achieve the results you want. You will need information on who you want the site to reach, what you want to say, and what is important to your target audience. Consider the following points for each type of site.

1. Organization site

Your organization site should provide information on —

    (a) who you are,

    (b) what you do,

    (c) your company's background/credibility, and

    (d) an overview of products or services.

It should be a continuing source of information about your organization and a facility for initial and continuing interaction.

2. Product site

A product site will provide the same information and services as an organization site, with some additional services —

    (a) who you are,

    (b) what you do,

    (c) background/credibility information,

    (d) detailed information on products or services,

    (e) continuing source of information about products/services,

    (f) on-line customer service, and

    (g) facility for initial and continuing interaction

3. Event or promotion site

An event or promotion site will list —

    (a) a description of the event or promotion,

    (b) its time and duration, and

    (c) detailed description and information.

The site will be a continuing source of information about the event or promotion and a facility for inquiries, comments, or bookings.

b. YOUR OBJECTIVE IN CREATING THE SITE

What is your primary objective in creating this site? You are going to invest time and money creating a Web site, and to make that investment pay, you must know the site's objectives. These objectives are crucial to the initial planning process and are essential for the review process later. Your site is the beginning of an on-line presence in the marketplace that will likely evolve and expand over time. The first step is to establish and focus on a clear, achievable goal — one you can see results from in a defined period.

An example of a clear objective is:

> The primary objective of the site is service and support. The site will provide first-level technical support information to our existing customers and is expected to reduce telephone support calls by approximately 10% in the first year of operation.

c. YOUR SITE'S MESSAGE

What message should your site deliver? This depends a great deal on the objective you have established for the site. The message will be communicated not only by the words themselves but also through the impressions created by the entire site.

d. ESTABLISHED IMAGES

Are there existing messages or established images that must be incorporated into the Web site? Is your company conservative, innovative, leading edge, people oriented, or service oriented? Will the site reflect the established or desired image of your company? What messages (image, identity, the message you want your site to convey, and the image you want your site to generate) are communicated through other marketing vehicles of your company, and how should the Web site be used to reinforce these messages?

TIP:

Take the time to review the Web sites of your competitors and of related businesses. What is it that you like about these sites, and what don't you like?

e. A CRITICAL LAUNCH DATE

Is there a critical date for launching your Web site? If there is, identify a launch target date early in the planning process. If the target date is critical because of a commitment or deadline, for example, let everyone involved with creating the Web site know.

f. DEFINING SUCCESS OR FAILURE

How are you going to define and quantify the success or failure of your Web site? If you cannot easily determine this, return to the task of defining site objectives.

In our example objective, success or failure may be determined by evaluating the customer's acceptance of the on-line support service, the effectiveness of the site content, and ultimately, the reduction of telephone support. The tools used to measure success might include a customer survey, a usage counter placed on the support pages, or telephone support records.

g. MAINTAINING THE SITE

Who will be responsible for maintaining the site? Effective Web sites require an ongoing commitment to change, enhancement, and management. It is important to establish early in the planning process who will be responsible for the site.

As well, who will be responsible for promoting the site? Although effective on-line promotion has become critical to the success of any Web site, this requirement is often overlooked. Read chapter 9 to get a better understanding of this key requirement.

You are now ready to begin the process of planning the infrastructure and content of your Web site. In upcoming sections, you will be using other worksheets and the Web Site Planning Map to create a definitive Web site plan.

2 WEB SITE PRODUCTION

Although you don't need to make a final decision right now about how you will be producing the Web site, you should be considering your options as you plan and design your site. Doing so will also help you as you create your Web site budget (see chapter 3).

A successful Web presence requires —

(a) good planning,

(b) effective design,

(c) competent technical production,

(d) dependable hosting, and

(e) promotion, promotion, promotion.

Once you have completed your Web site plan, you will be ready to move on to the actual Web site production process. This process melds the text, graphics, forms, underlying scripts, utilities, and services together to create a Web site.

The production process (sometimes referred to as HTML authoring) uses a software package called a Web editor to create HTML (hypertext markup language) pages. HTML is similar in function to word processing software, as it adds function-specific codes to text and graphics to create organized output. Unlike a word processor, which is designed to produce hard copy output, HTML produces screen-based documents that may be viewed by any Web browser that conforms to recognized HTML standards and conventions.

You will need to make two key decisions before you begin the technical production process: who will do the technical development and who will host your site? Keep these questions in mind as you continue through the planning and design stages of your Web site development, so that you are ready to make these decisions once the first stages are completed.

a. TECHNICAL DEVELOPMENT

First, who is going to do the technical development? Will the technical site development be done in your organization or will you hire an external Web site production service?

1. Developing your Web site in-house

The production of HTML pages is not rocket science, but, like anything else, it requires practice and the successful application of basic skills to produce quality output. If you are contemplating the technical production of your own Web pages, consider the following:

(a) What software and hardware are required and available to do the job? Take the time to research Web editors and Web site development software packages.

(b) What resource time is available? Be sure to allow sufficient time for a reasonable learning curve in your production schedule.

(c) What is the target time frame for development of the site?

(d) How does the cost, convenience, and output quality of an internally produced Web site compare with an external alternative?

(e) How important is developing internal Web production resources?

As well, you should —

(a) speak to others who have produced their own Web sites about their in-house development;

(b) ensure that the marketing/communication objectives of the site dictate the end product, rather than allowing available technology to dictate the design of your site;

(c) compare your site plan with those of your competitors or with sites you admire, and do not launch your site until you are confident you have attained a similar level of quality; and

(d) consider using the services of an external resource for the production of scripts, animation, or any portion of the development that lies outside your skills.

The plan and material you compile during the planning and design processes will prepare you to properly evaluate your production alternatives. As well, the detailed Web site plan can be used as a specifications document that you give to external Web site development and/or hosting services to obtain a binding quotation on production or hosting services.

2. Using an external Web site development service

If you plan to use an external Web production service, consider the following:

- What other organizations use its services?
- Do any of your competitors use its services?
- Are you happy with the quality of other sites that it has produced?
- Can it meet your targets?
- Is it likely to be in business next year?
- Is the pricing competitive based on desired quality?
- What are its payment terms?
- What is its correction/guarantee policy?
- How much will updates cost?
- How can you optimize the update process?
- Does the external production house use anything that may limit your freedom to locate the site on any server environment or use any facilities? For example, does the developer use Web authoring tools that require server facilities to handle non-standard extensions? Does it use server-specific search and/or database facilities or vendor-specific facilities or conventions?

This book will help you plan and design your Web site. It contains worksheets to assist you in gathering the information you will want when you begin planning and designing your Web site, and provides instruction on developing the Web site in-house. As well, the author's company offers a service to readers who want assistance in getting up and running on the Web once they have completed their planning worksheets. More details about this service are provided in Appendix 3.

If you decide to use an external service, you will be able to find potential production companies through the following sources:

(a) *Word of mouth.* Ask friends, colleagues, and associates if they can recommend any Internet service providers.

(b) *The World Wide Web.* See if any of the local companies you recognize have Web Sites. If they do and you like the way their Web site functions, see who developed the site (the developer is usually named on the site itself or on the source pages of the site).

(c) *The Yellow Pages.* Look under the heading Internet and read the ads to determine which companies focus on Web-based services. You will save considerable time by avoiding those companies which focus exclusively on connectivity and e-mail services.

(d) *Advertisements in local papers, magazines, and trade or computer papers.*

These suggestions will also help you if you decide to look for an external hosting facility (see section **b.**).

b. HOSTING YOUR WEB SITE

In a few short days, you will have a completed Web site. The next key decision is determining who will host your site. Investigate your options and decide which best meets your requirements. Selecting a hosting facility *now* is important because it may affect which Web site services will be supported, which scripts and utilities can be present, and possibly which extensions will be supported (some Web site development packages produce HTML with non-standard extensions that may not be supported on some servers). A well-managed, high-speed, Web-hosting organization will ensure accessibility of your information to the Web community. You have three main options.

1. Internal server

Your organization may host your Web site on its own internal server connected to the Internet. This option requires that you invest in computer hardware, software, communications resources, and expertise. Very large companies or organizations with special requirements or considerations tend to choose this option.

2. Dedicated server at a third-party facility

You may choose to place your Web site on a server dedicated to your use at a third-party facility offering shared access to the Internet. This option offers: reduced cost for high-speed Internet connections; added security (because the server is physically separate from your business's information processing systems); and the opportunity to share technical and support resources. It is still an expensive option for many organizations, as they often will not make full use of the resources of a dedicated server.

3. Commercial organizations providing shared hosting services

Numerous commercial organizations specifically provide hosting services and Internet connectivity. These organizations offer clients services that usually exceed the level of service an average company could offer through a dedicated server for the same cost.

Many of the organizations offering these services are ISPs, or Internet service providers, that have traditionally focused on connectivity services. Other organizations are now appearing that primarily provide sophisticated hosting services for commercial clients.

If you go this route, be careful which company you choose. Here are some guidelines:

(a) *Determine what the company's charter really is.* If its primary focus is not the provision of hosting services, the ongoing commitment to state-of-the-art services may be absent. This is important since you may at some time need audio, video, database, financial transaction processing, and numerous other related services for your site. Your ability to use these services will be limited by the services provided by that company.

(b) *One-stop shopping may not be the answer for your company's Internet needs.* The local organization that provides Internet connectivity and e-mail services may not be the best source for hosting services. It is common to have access and e-mail services supplied by one organization and hosting services supplied by another. If you plan to use a registered domain name, the domain name may be contained in your Web site's uniform resource locator (URL) and your organization's e-mail addresses without complications, even though the companies providing you with e-mail services and Web hosting services are hundreds of miles apart. Your server's geographical location is unimportant. What is important is the speed and reliability of the server's resources and the high-speed link to the Internet.

(c) *Using a registered domain name has its advantages but also its costs.* You are the best judge of the value of immediately using a domain name (e.g., *www.yourco.com*). Register your domain name regardless of whether you will use it immediately or not. Domain names will only be harder to acquire the longer you wait, and the initial registration cost and annual fees are nominal.

For most companies, the domain name will not be the primary source of visibility on the Web. Visibility comes from proactive promotion and the use of intelligent keywords and site descriptions (see chapter 9, section **b.**, for a discussion of keywords). Unless you are a leader in your industry, the world at large will not initially find you by keying *www.yourco.com*.

It usually costs more to have your Web site hosted as a full domain (e.g., *www.yourco.com*) on a Web server than being hosted as a shared domain on a server (e.g., *www.serverco.com/yourco*). If cost is a major criterion in the initial stages of your Web site development, you may want to consider the following strategy:

(1) Register your domain name immediately.

(2) Use the domain name in your e-mail addresses.

(3) Have your server company host you visibly under its shared domain (e.g., *www.serverco.com/yourco*).

(4) When you choose to be hosted as a full domain, your server company can implement a pointer from the shared address to your new address so that bookmarks will continue to be functional.

The information in chapter 3 will help you analyze the costs of developing your Web site and may make it easier for you to decide whether to go with in-house or out-of-house development and hosting.

3 HOW MUCH WILL IT COST?

A well-designed Web site has the potential to provide tremendous value for your investment dollar. Regardless of this potential, it is very important for all companies, and especially small companies, to recognize all costs associated with the initiative. Costs may include software, hardware, services, and direct staff costs. Be aware of all actual costs early and base your decisions and timeline on your financial reality. It is better to build a well-designed, smaller site than to try to cut corners on larger sites.

It is a good idea to read through this book first so that you have a better sense of the process before you begin working on your budget.

Worksheet #2, the Web Site Budget Planner (see Appendix 1), provides a comprehensive list of factors to include in a realistic budget. As you determine your actual costs, you must realize the value of your time and of all other internal resources. Don't fall into the trap of considering internal resource time as free. Sample #2 shows a model budget.

TIP:

Be sure to consider any existing marketing or business materials as a resource within this process. Save money and time by using existing content and design whenever possible.

a. PLANNING/DESIGN

By following the *Winning Web Sites* step-by-step process to plan and design your own Web page, you could potentially save hundreds of dollars. At the same time, you will have a direct impact on the quality of your Web site because of your hands-on involvement. Compare the cost of planning in-house, using this book, to the cost of using an outside service.

13

b. DEVELOPMENT/PRODUCTION

The development/production phase is where your completed Web site plan is transformed into one or more electronic files which, when viewed by a browser — a tool used to read HTML documents — appear as a Web page or pages. The production process requires the authoring of HTML (hypertext markup language) pages. You have two production alternatives: you can create the Web site yourself, or you can use a commercial Web production service (discussed in chapter 2).

1. Do it yourself

Create the Web pages using a Web editor or one of the several Web page creation packages available at your local computer store. Consider the following: How much will it cost you in terms of your own or your staff's time? Do you have the available time? Do you have all the hardware and software necessary to process text, photos, and graphics? If not, how much will it cost to buy the proper material? Do you have the design skills to achieve the desired result or will you need to hire freelancers or temporary staff to help at certain points? How much will that cost?

2. Use a Web production service

Many small companies may find it more convenient, faster, and more effective to take the completed Web site plan to a Web production service than to do it themselves. Determine the cost, the quality of that company's previous work, how long the company has been in business, and its ability to work with your selected hosting service.

c. HOSTING

Once completed, you will want your Web site to be available 24 hours a day to anyone who looks for it. Web site hosting refers to the storage of your electronic Web page on a specialized computer system continuously connected to the Internet.

Since you want people who seek your business out on the Internet to get to it quickly and consistently, you'll want to store your Web site on a reliable, fast Web server. Reliability and speed of access are two qualities that should not be compromised when choosing a server. The server fee, like your telephone cost, is a basic cost of delivering your message to the world through a Web site. Chapter 2 discusses Web site hosting in more detail. It is something you need to consider as you prepare your Web site budget.

d. ON-LINE AND OTHER PROMOTION

The use and management of search engines, lists, indexes, and other forms of on-line and off-line promotion are fundamental ingredients to your site's success. The success of your Web site depends on both the quality and visibility of the site. The more hours spent efficiently promoting your site, the greater its visibility on the Web and to your target audience. I suggest you spend a minimum of 15 hours on promotion during the first six weeks of operation. Or you can farm this task out to an external resource. More details on Web site promotion are available in chapter 9.

e. CONTENT UPDATES

Once your Web site has been launched, the process of updating and maintaining your site begins. A site must be available and functioning properly to be effective; the information at the site must also be accurate and timely.

Estimate the approximate number of hours per month required to make basic content changes to your site. To do this, you need to determine what content is subject to change and how often that change is likely to occur. If changes are limited to simple text alterations, the time required to update the Web site is approximately one and a half times what is required to make a textual change within a word processing document. This allows for time to make the change and upload the changes to the server.

But you do need to be clear on when a change is a change and when it is actually an expansion or a reworking of the site. To determine the cost of this, you must estimate the following:

(a) How often will changes be required?

(b) What graphic and textual changes will be required?

(c) How long will it take to implement the changes?

(d) What will the resources cost to accomplish these changes?

The cost of an update ranges dramatically depending on whether there are only simple text changes or whether updates include extensive text, graphic, or structural changes. For the purpose of this budget, you may wish to estimate the cost of basic content changes only.

TIP:

If you consider your time free, you may want to review your rates. Your time and that of your associates is probably your most limited resource. Place the appropriate value on it.

f. MAINTENANCE

Web site maintenance is the work of keeping your Web site current with the general level of quality and sophistication found within Web sites of similar size and focus. The technologies and techniques associated with Web site development and management are rapidly changing, resulting in the rapid dating of Web sites that do not change with these new facilities. A Web site should be reviewed and renewed at least once a year.

If your site stays approximately the same size and does not need additional technology services, the cost associated with maintaining the site on an annual basis, at a level consistent with the general state of the Web, is approximately 30% of the original design and production costs. This percentage may be higher for very small sites and lower for larger sites.

g. FIRST YEAR WEB SITE BUDGET

The final section of the Budget Planner will help you calculate the cost for the first year's operation of your Web site. This will provide you with a realistic figure for an effective business site, so you can avoid any unpleasant financial surprises in this project.

Planning/Design

(Based upon a commercial quality five-page site with one interactive form.)

Option A — In-house Planning Activities

Resource Material	$ 60
Staff Cost	1,600 based upon 40 staff participation hours
Option A Total	$ 1,660

-or-

Option B — External Planning Services

External Resource Fee	$ _____
Staff Cost	_____ based upon ___ staff participation hours
Option B Total	$ _____

Development/Production Costs

Option A — In-house Site Production

Resource Materials	$_____
Staff Cost	_____ based upon ___ staff participation hours
Option A Total	$_____

-or-

Option B — External Site Production

Production Fee	$ 800
Staff Cost	120 based upon 3 staff participation hours
Option B Total	$ 920

Hosting

Option A — Internal Web Site Hosting

Hardware Costs	$_____/mo.
Software Costs	_____/mo.
Telecommunications Costs	_____/mo.
Staff Costs	_____/mo.
Other Costs	_____/mo.
Option A Total	$_____/mo.

17

-or-

Option B — External Web Site Hosting

Hosting Fee	$ __60/mo.__	based upon a monthly fee of $__60__
Staff Cost	__80/mo.__	based upon __2__ staff participation hours
Option B Total	$ __140/mo.__	

On-line Promotion

You should plan on spending a minimum of 15 hours for on-line promotion of your Web site within the first 6 weeks of operation. This is only a suggested minimum. The success of your Web site is dependent upon both the quality and visibility of the site. The more hours spent efficiently promoting your Web site should result in greater visibility on the Web and within your targeted audience.

Option A — Promotional Costs — In-house Resources

Promotion $ __600__   based upon __20__ staff hrs. of promotion
                   at $__30__/hr.

-or-

Option B — Promotional Costs — External Resources

Promotion $ _____   based upon ____ hrs. of promotion
                   at $___/hr.

Other Promotion

Production and placement of promotional banners within commercial sites $ __N/A__
Use of commercial listing services $ __N/A__
Direct cost of additional advertising of the Web site in other media $__75__/mo.

Content Updates

For budgeting purposes, estimate the approximate number of hours per month required to facilitate basic content changes. The first step is to determine what content is subject to change and how often that change is likely to occur. If changes are limited to simple text changes, the time required to perform the updates to the Web site is approximately 1.5 times the period required to make a textual change within a word processing document. This allows for resource time required to make the change and upload the changes to the server.

Estimated monthly resource hours for updates _____1_____

Estimated monthly cost of updates based upon _____1_____ resource hours

at $__45____/hour = $__45____

Maintenance

Web site maintenance refers to the cost associated with keeping your Web site current with the general level of quality and sophistication found within Web sites of similar size and focus. The technologies and techniques associated with Web site development and management are rapidly changing, resulting in the rapid dating of Web sites that do not change with these new facilities. You should review and renew your Web site at least once a year. If your site stays approximately the same size and does not require the introduction of additional technology services, the cost associated with maintaining the site on an annual basis, at a level consistent with the general state of the Web, is estimated to be approximately 30% of the original design and production costs. This percentage may be higher for very small sites and lower for larger sites.

Estimated maintenance cost based upon the information above $____500_____

First Year Web Site Budget

	In-house	External
Planning/Design Costs	$ 1,660	$
Development/Production Costs		920
Hosting Fees		1,680
On-line Promotion Fees	600	
Other Promotional Fees		900
Content Updating Fees		540
Maintenance Fees		500
Total first year Web site cost (including internal staff costs)	$ 2,260	+ $ 4,540 = $ **6,800**

N.B. The above budget reflects a decision to complete the planning process in-house and to use external resources for Production, Hosting, Promotion, Updating and Maintenance. Prices will vary from one company to another. See Appendix 3 for additional examples of pricing.

4
PROCESS AND CONTENT

a. PRELIMINARY PLANNING

At the preliminary stage of the Web site planning process, you'll organize the who, what, where, and when of your Web site. Worksheet #3, the Content Planner (see Appendix 1), will help you keep track of your planning and design team (even if that team is just made up of you) and will provide you with an overview of what resources are required, where those resources are coming from, and when you have received them. Sample #3 shows you a filled-in Content Planner that will give you a sense of what information you will have to gather. But don't worry if you are unable to complete the form for your own company at this instant. If you are not yet clear what content you want for your site, or what types of pages you should use, continue reading through this chapter and chapters 5 and 6. These chapters will provide you with much more detailed information about content options, and then you can go back to the Content Planner with a better sense of how to fill it in.

1. Project contributors

Even with a one-person planning team, other people may contribute resources to building your Web site. The person who printed your business cards might supply a copy of a logo, or a good amateur photographer might contribute some photos. These sources need to be tracked for your own records and also for issues of copyright. To stay on top of this, ask yourself:

   (a) Who will be involved in building the Web site?

   (b) What will each person contribute and what is the degree of his or her involvement?

(c) What is the target time frame for the planning phase?

(d) What is the target date for having a live site?

If you are the sole member of a one-person project team, go ahead and fill in Section A of the Content Planner — details of the preliminary planning meeting. Refer to Sample #3 for guidance.

If you are coordinating or leading a project team, review the planning stage as a whole (by reading through the book) and then create an agenda for the first project team meeting. The objective of this meeting will be to determine most of the information and resources needed for building your site. Fill in Section A of the Content Planner during your preliminary planning meeting or as early in the process as possible.

You should already have defined the objectives, intent, message, and audience of your Web site when you completed the Site Preplanner (see Worksheet #1 in Appendix 1 and Sample #1 in chapter 1), but it's worth revisiting the Preplanner at this stage, especially if you will be working with other people who might have different perspectives on any of these issues. Get as many ideas from outside sources as possible during the planning process; you can evaluate the merit of each later.

2. Images and text required

The information to be recorded in the "Photos/Images required" and "Text/Copy required" portions of the Content Planner will be finalized as the creative process evolves, but try to fill in as much as you can at this point. Remember that you can always change what you have written down as ideas for the site crystallize; think of the Planner as a living document — malleable, not fixed.

3. Web site structure

If you are able, at this point record the type of Web site you will create (organization, product, or event/special promotion — information perhaps already determined when you completed

TIP:

The Site Preplanner and the other planning documents are needed at various points throughout the design process. Carefully tear them out of Appendix 1 and keep them together in a folder or envelope, ready for quick reference. Sometimes parts of the planning documents will need to be completed after you have finished later stages of the design process.

your Site Preplanner), the number of pages the Web site will have, and the type of Web pages to be included.

b. WHAT GOES WHERE?
CONTENT PLANNING PROCESS

Section B of the Content Planner will help you organize text elements in the Web site. It will assist you in sorting out the types of Web pages you should use, the links between the pages, and the graphic and text file names you will associate with each page. After you have decided in general terms what content will go where, you will be ready to design the infrastructure of the site. This process is described in detail in chapter 6.

1. Graphics: input and output

Graphics make an important contribution to the appearance and effectiveness of a Web site. If you understand how Web site developers process and display graphics, you will be able to avoid unnecessary complications or misunderstandings in planning your Web site.

Graphics may include photographs, illustrations, charts, logos, and drawings. It is important to remember that the graphic will be displayed in a compact form on a computer screen with a resolution of 72 dots per inch (dpi). Detailed drawings and maps are likely to lose much of their value unless a Zoom Page is used. (A Zoom Page displays a larger version of the image, usually approaching screen size. It is accessed by clicking on a smaller version of the image on a standard Web page.)

Although technology allows you to place an unlimited number of photos or graphic elements on any one page, you may want to consider limiting the number of major graphics per page for efficiency and to keep costs down. You can always add more graphics later, once you have tested and developed your site. To begin with, it is recommended that you use only one or two graphics per page (excluding design accents). Your graphics might include a combination of logos, photographs, and illustrations.

Graphics may be processed from hard copy materials (scanned) or as a graphics file on a 3.5" diskette in either PC or Macintosh format. Hard copy alternatives include photographs (5" x 7" images yield the best results, but snapshot size is acceptable), pictures from printed brochures or catalogues (the image should be at least 2" x 2" to allow a quality capture), logos or illustrations (high density, high quality images are always preferred), and any other hard copy image that will allow reasonable capture on a quality flatbed scanner. Electronic files are

TIP:

You have the opportunity to create an effective first impression for the Web community. Be careful to ensure that the impression you create reflects how you want others to perceive your organization.

commonly acceptable in TIF, GIF, BMP, PSD, PCX, and JPG formats. Slides or transparencies usually require additional processing at extra cost. For logos I recommend you use a PMT with color specifications, although a logo from existing print material is usually acceptable.

Since the standard output display density is approximately 72 dpi, the following graphics display sizes for your Web pages will ensure optimum efficiency, quality, and consistency of output. These sizes are approximate and should be considered as recommendations only — check with your Web production house before proceeding:

- ID Page: 3.5" x 2"
- Combo Page: 2.75" x 1.75"
- Zoom Page: 5.5" x 3.25"
- All other pages: 2.75" x 1.75"

2. Text input

The majority of content in your Web site is likely to be text. All text copy should be well organized, grammatically correct, and spell checked. The amount of text contained on any page will vary significantly by page type. Usually an ID Page has very limited text, while Detail Pages contain the most text. In general, you should attempt to achieve a balance between text, graphics, and open space on your Web pages.

Take the time to organize and edit your message so it is communicated clearly and succinctly. Web users appreciate being able to choose what they see and the level of information they read. Move from general to detailed information by using links in your pages. When you develop Web pages, you are usually charged by the number of pages input, not by the number of screens output, so use those links!

Many Web site developers use the standard page size of 8.5" x 11" to measure input for Web site production. The content of the Web page is equivalent to what can fit on one standard page with a margin of 0.5" on all sides and text in a 12-point font, single spaced (approximately 3,000 characters per page if text only).

Although text-only pages may seem a good value, most Web pages will require some graphic elements for visual appeal, to better communicate the message, and to provide a pleasant browsing environment. Remember your audience, your objective, and your message!

Most Web site developers measure output in screen lengths. As a general rule, one standard input page will equal 2.5 browser screen lengths of information. Unlike most hard copy

TIP:

Don't rely on your software program's spell checker to catch all typos. Spell checkers will catch misspelled words, but they won't catch instances when "from" is used instead of "form," etc. Read through your text carefully, and get someone else with a fresh pair of eyes to do so as well.

mediums, a Web browser displays content in a landscape mode with a broader horizontal than vertical display. Because of this feature, and because a portion of the screen is taken up by the Web browser command line, the reader usually has to scroll vertically, and in many cases horizontally, to view the contents of the Web or screen page. There is one exception: the highly graphic ID Page tends to be designed to fit one screen length for user convenience and visual impact (see chapter 5 for a description of the different types of Web pages).

Develop your content to create a pleasant viewing environment; strive to achieve a balance between text, graphics, and white space. Users of the Web want to quickly establish what information is available and of interest to them in your site. Then they want to determine the importance and quality of the information and conveniently access further detail if desired. The flow of most popular Web sites is designed to move from site overview, to summary, to detail.

Quality and effectiveness should be the foundations of your Web site. Quality, not size, will dictate success. Over time, your Web presence may be expanded and funded from the site's success.

3. Preparing text

The text for each page should be typed or clearly printed and labeled with the corresponding page type and number. If possible, save the text segment as ASCII text files and give each file a name that refers to its associated page. This way, no matter how your site is produced — in-house or by an external production house — your text and electronic text files will be clearly laid out. Use Section B of the Content Planner to plan your own text inventory and keep track of files and links. Although you may not be able to complete this section immediately, keep it handy as you complete the worksheets for each Web site page type (see chapter 7) and record the information on the text inventory record as you go.

4. Hypertext links

If you want information to be accessible by a hypertext link from within a Web page, simply highlight the text to be contained in the link by underlining the word(s) that will trigger or activate the link. For example, if you want the first instance of the word "accessible" in this paragraph to be a hypertext trigger to a link having the text, "We present your organization to the world," you would include that second sentence of text

TIP:

One textual element of a Web page is a wordmark. A wordmark is a particular way of displaying a name or a phrase to identify a company or product. Many small companies do not have logos but instead use stylized wordmarks. For example, John Smith Realty may always want its wordmark to be John Smith Realty displayed in bold, italicized, 20-point Arial font.

<u>SECTION A</u> Preliminary planning meeting

Date: <u>May 1, 199-</u>

Attendees: <u>Sam, Bob, Geoff</u>

Primary person/team: <u>Sam, Bob, Geoff</u>

Target deadline for receiving images and text: <u>May 10, 199-</u>

Web site type: <u>Product</u>

Web site size (number of input pages): <u>6 pages</u>

Page types to be included (see chapter 5):

<u>ID Page, Detail Page, Form Page, Links Page, and Zoom Page</u>

Photos/images required

	Description	Page no.	Source	Date req'd	Date rec'd	X
1.	Pearlsea logo	1	Marketing - Sam	05/03	05/03	☒
2.	Trays	2	Photo - Sam	05/03	05/03	☒
3.	Boxes	2	Photo - Sam	05/03	05/03	☒
4.	Scenic photo	3	Photo - Sam	05/03	05/03	☒
5.	Logo:Pearl Bay	4	Logo - Sam	05/03	05/03	☒
6.	Logo:Summer	4	Logo - Sam	05/03	05/03	☒
7.						☐
8.						☐
9.						☐
10.						☐

Text/Copy required

	Description	Page no.	Source	Date req'd	Date rec'd	X
1.	Site summary	1 ID page	Geoff	05/05	05/05	☒
2.	Ranching info	2	Existing brochure	05/05	05/05	☒
3.	Recipe info	3	Existing & new (Sam)	05/05	05/05	☒
4.	Pearl Bay info	4	Existing brochure	05/05	05/05	☒
5.	Summer Ice info	4	Existing brochure	05/05	05/05	☒
6.	Order form text	5	Bob to create	05/08	05/08	☒
7.	Links list	6	Sam, Bob & Geoff	05/10	05/10	☒
8.						☐
9.						☐
10.						☐

Fill in the following if applicable:

Date package sent to production company: May 15, 199- via: ☐ mail ☐ courier

Anticipated site completion date: June 1, 199-

SECTION B Text inventory record

Page 1	Page type: ID	File name: PS.IDB.txt
Page 2	Page type: Detail	File name: PS.D27.txt
Page 3	Page type: Detail	File name: PS.D37.txt
Page 4	Page type: Detail	File name: PS.D47.txt
Page 5	Page type: Order	File name: PS.ordfm.txt
Page 6	Page type: Links page	File name: PS.Linkp.txt
Page 7	Page type: Zoom page	File name: PS.zoom.txt
Link page 1	Linked from page:	Link word/phrase:
Link page 2	Linked from page:	Link word/phrase:
Link page 3	Linked from page:	Link word/phrase:
Link page 4	Linked from page:	Link word/phrase:
Link page 5	Linked from page:	Link word/phrase:
Link page 6	Linked from page:	Link word/phrase:
Link page 7	Linked from page:	Link word/phrase:
Link page 8	Linked from page:	Link word/phrase:
Link page 9	Linked from page:	Link word/phrase:
Link page 10	Linked from page:	Link word/phrase:

on the page containing the trigger word(s) and indicate the link as: <u>accessible</u>. The linked content is measured within the content page on which it is typed but is displayed on a separate output screen activated by the trigger word.

c. ASSEMBLING AND ORGANIZING YOUR WEB SITE'S CONTENT

You have been introduced to a considerable amount of information that will prepare you to plan your Web site infrastructure and content in a knowledgeable, professional way. Now it's up to you to assemble the Web site content required to meet the objectives of your site.

Review your Site Preplanner (Worksheet #1) and Content Planner (Worksheet #3), and briefly look at the worksheets that you'll find in chapter 7, to determine what content you will need for production. Then determine what content you already have. This is a first-pass attempt at assembling potential content, so don't be overly selective at this time; material can be pared down later on in the process. Common sources of content include:

- Corporate or product brochures and information sheets
- Presentation materials from your company or from similar companies or suppliers
- Proposal or bid documents
- Advertising materials

After making a first pass to assemble existing content, take a look at what you have found. Determine how much of the existing material can be used in the Web site given the objectives of your site. Establish what can be used as is, what needs to be updated, what needs to be rewritten or modified, and what is of no value.

As the information is assembled in logical units and in a logical sequence, you will need to ask yourself: What graphics are required for communicating and for adding visual interest? What detail copy is still required? Are there obvious gaps in content or presented information?

At this point, most teams find that they require additional content. This can be found in a number of places including:

- A second pass at internal sources
- Suppliers, customers, and associated organizations
- Industry participants and respected competitors — be careful to use concepts, not actual content

- New material specifically created for use within the Web site

Once all the raw data is collected, the next step is to determine how best to present the information within the Web site. Compare your content information with the Web site page types presented in chapters 5 and 6 of this book; this should prepare you for completing the worksheets required to produce your site (see chapter 7). As you begin to complete these worksheets, you will become increasingly aware of the necessity to organize content elements. It is extremely important that you read and understand chapter 7 before you begin this process.

TIP:

As you assemble and organize content, there is great potential for misplacing documents. Create a folder to store all the materials. Place an envelope inside the folder to hold all graphics materials. It's amazing how much paper and other material you'll handle in the planning and development process.

5 HOW IS INFORMATION ORGANIZED?
TYPICAL WEB SITES
AND THE WEB SITE
PLANNING MAP

This chapter provides you with a broad overview of how to organize information in a typical Web site. The term "typical Web site" is used rather loosely here because there are an infinite number of ways to plan a Web site and to structure and combine its component parts. What follows is a basic structure which you can build on as you become more comfortable with the planning process.

First, you will learn about the different page types commonly found in a Web site. Names are given to these page types for the sake of clarity, but this terminology (e.g., ID Page, Detail Page, Links Page) is not universally used by all production houses or Web site builders. The Web production house that you use will have labels to keep the content components organized in its planning process. As you work with your production house, you may find they use different terminology. But they should still be able to work with your plans.

Chapter 6 describes how to plan these page types in more detail and provides filled-in samples of the various page types on the Web Site Planning Map. Chapter 7 will lead you through the worksheets for planning each individual page.

Now that you have roughly determined what you want your site to communicate (by using the Site Preplanner, Content Planner, and by gathering additional information as you read the previous chapters), it's time to assess which Web page types will accommodate your compiled information. The following explanations of each page type will help you structure your Web site page layout.

Other than page one, which is usually an ID Page or a Combo Page (often called a Home Page), subsequent pages in your site may be any combination of Detail, Form, or other special purpose pages (e.g., Table Pages, Zoom Pages) depending on the purpose of your site. See Table #1 for a brief summary of page types and how Web pages can connect in a site.

Depending on the amount of content you wish to include, the purpose of your site (i.e., whether it's an organization site, a product site, or an event site), and the site size, you may choose one or more of these Web page types. However, while you are planning, remember that as the size of your files increases, so do your production costs. Also, the more graphics you include (and the more sophisticated those graphics are), the larger your files are going to be and the longer it will take for someone to download your Web pages. If the downloading takes too long, you may lose a potential customer.

a. PAGE 1

1. ID Page

The ID Page is designed to be visually appealing and interesting to a target audience. This page is very similar to a book cover in that it greatly influences whether the viewer proceeds or reads further in the Web site. The ID Page contains a logo or photograph to help readers identify the organization whose site

FIGURE # 1
ID PAGE
This Web site's ID Page bears a logo to establish the company's image.

32

TABLE #1
PAGE TYPE SUMMARY

Page Type	Position	Purpose	Comments
ID Page	Page 1	Graphical page — must convey identity, impact, and interest	Similar to a book cover — image oriented, limited text. Need to balance graphical requirement with download efficiency.
Combo Page	Page 1	Combines identity and site content	Similar to the ID Page in its role of identity page, but this page type tends to be less visual and moves directly into content presentation.
Detail Page	As required	Basic presentation page, summary/detail	The Detail Page is the most common page type and may be used to present all information that is not related to forms. It should be viewed as a multi-purpose "blank" page that is extremely flexible. It may contain columns or tables.
Table Page	As required	Tabular presentation of information	This page is similar in purpose to the Detail Page. However, it has been created with the purpose of presenting information in tables containing rows and columns.
Zoom Page	As required	A page used to show an expanded view	This page allows a visitor to see an enlarged or expanded view of a graphical element within the site that has been linked to a Zoom Page. The Zoom Page may include text content in addition to the enlarged graphic. Zoom Pages allow users to determine which large graphics they choose to view while allowing the basic content pages to load efficiently.
Database Interface Page	As required	Allows a database query to be entered	This is a specialized page that facilitates a database query. This page may only be used if the Web site is linked to a Web-based database application.
Search Page	As required	Allows a search of the Web site contents	This is a specialized page that facilitates a Web site search. This page may only be used if the Web site is linked to a Web-based search application.
Form Page	As required	On-line form supporting orders or interaction with Web site visitors	An interactive form facilitating the transmission of product orders, comments, and/or questions from a Web site visitor to a predefined e-mail address. This form encourages information exchange and serves to initiate communication between the parties.
Links Page	As required	Page listing active links to external sites	This page is used to provide a convenient list of links to external sites which have been selected by the site authors. Usually these sites contain related information or content that is of interest to the Web site's target audience.

they are visiting, and it very often provides a brief Web site summary statement. This page also includes essential links and site navigation facilities (i.e., links to Detail Pages).

2. Combo Page

Like the ID Page, the Combo Page creates a first impression for the on-line visitor. The Combo Page contains a logo or photograph for identity purposes and a larger text component than that found on the ID Page. This text component is likely to be a more detailed summary statement or an immediate entry into detailed product or service information.

FIGURE #2
COMBO PAGE

This Combo Page makes a quick transition from establishing the company's identity to providing detail about the company.

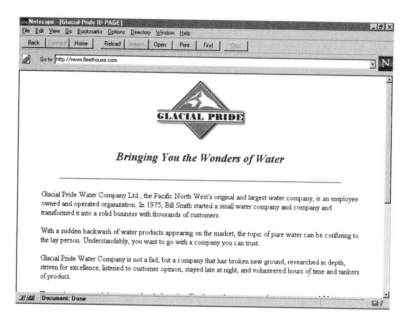

b. PAGE 2 OR 2+: DETAIL PAGES

A Detail Page will likely be used in every Web site. A Detail Page delivers a message through the display of text and graphics in a traditional layout similar to what may be seen in a conventional brochure or magazine. There is usually a page header, one or two graphics, and accompanying text. Provisions must be made for simple navigational capabilities — for example, you may want to provide an alternate page with no pictures for browsers that are not capable of reading graphics. Detail Pages can be organized by general subject content, but the structure will differ depending on what type of site you choose.

1. Organization or product site

The organization or product site may include pages covering a company overview, its products and services, or what's new or being planned for the future. The focus of the site is on a specific business or business product.

2. Event or special promotion site

An event or special promotion site may include pages giving an overview of an event, a schedule or promotion summary, a promotion detail, and other related information. If a special promotion is time sensitive, make sure that you are updating the information on the site to reflect these time constraints.

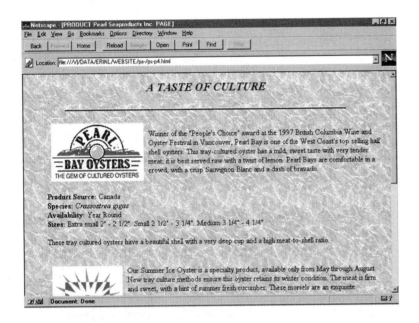

FIGURE #3
DETAIL PAGE

In this site, the Detail Page is used to give greater detail on the company's products.

3. Alternative to Detail Page

Depending on the type of site you are creating, you may choose to use an alternative to a Detail Page. Consider using one of these special purpose pages in conjunction with or in place of a standard Detail Page.

(a) Table Page

The Table Page, a variant of a Detail Page, employs a table (a configuration using rows and columns to organize content) to display information on the page.

A Table Page delivers a message by displaying text and graphics in a layout similar to what may be seen in a catalogue, product summary, or specification sheet. There is usually a page header, logo or identity graphic, and the table component containing a predefined number of rows and columns with text information in each cell. Provisions must be made for simple navigation capabilities.

If you choose to display information using tables, you should consider the visible screen width of a basic screen (640 x 480 pixels) when designing them. If the number and length of cells in each row are too great, a horizontal scroll will be necessary and all vertical information (columns) will not be visible at the same time. Many Internet users consider horizontal scrolling to be undesirable, whereas vertical scrolling is very common and well accepted.

Another thing to watch for is the number of vertical rows. If your input is measured by input pages, a larger number of rows will likely exceed a standard page and will take longer to load.

One last point to keep in mind is that although you could insert a table in a Form Page or a Detail Page or almost any other type of page, a Table Page consists primarily of one or more tables.

FIGURE #4
TABLE PAGE

A Table Page allows you to list information such as statistics in an easy-to-read format.

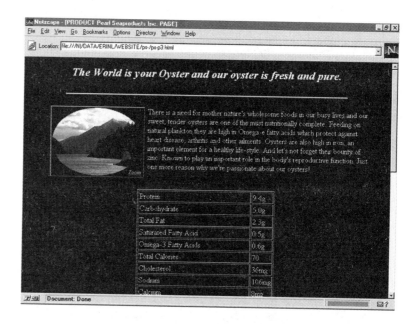

(b) Zoom Page

Many products, services, and events are best promoted through the use of appealing visuals. The Zoom Page is designed to address some of the challenges that exist when you attempt to deliver high-quality images over the Web.

Detailed maps and diagrams cannot be viewed effectively in small formats on a standard computer screen. The obvious solution of embedding larger, high-resolution images in a Web page is not viable because of the large file sizes of these images

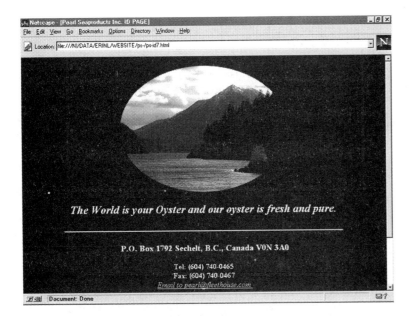

and the relatively slow data transfer rate (bandwidth) available to the majority of Web users.

The Zoom Page is useful because it allows users to selectively download larger images. The user selects only those images that he or she is interested in and prepared to wait for. The user makes this decision from a standard size image and/or descriptive text on, for example, a standard Detail Page. The enlarged image is usually sized to fit in a single browser screen without scrolling.

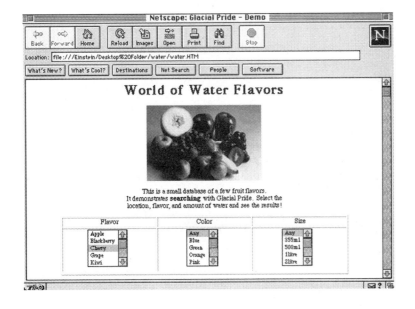

(c) Database Interface Page

A Database Interface Page is used only when a Web-accessible database has been developed. Databases tend to be client specific and therefore require customized development.

The Database Interface Page will only be used by those organizations requiring an integrated database facility within their Web site. These facilities are usually required when large amounts of information are present which must be sorted or qualified or otherwise processed quickly upon demand. An example of such a database might be a large and diverse product line that carries numerous products under a variety of categories.

The Database Interface worksheet and form (located in Appendix 2) fill a dual role. If your Web site production will be completed by an external production service, you will likely use the form twice, as you do the Search Page form. First, use it to communicate the database interface requirement to the production service to verify its ability to provide the interface at an acceptable price. Second, use the form as part of the Web site plan and submission package after the review/quotation process.

(d) Search Page

A Search Page requires that an integrated search facility be built into the Web site. Search facilities range from simple text searches to highly sophisticated searches for multiple qualifiers. Search capabilities are dependent on the host server. If you plan to have a Search Page, be sure to research this issue with prospective hosting services.

FIGURE #7
SEARCH PAGE
This Web page provides viewers with an interface that allows them to make inquiries.

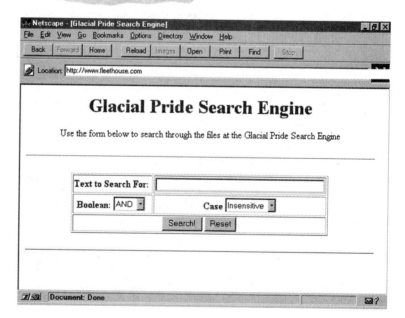

The Search Page provides users with a convenient way to initiate a text-based search of your Web site content. Don't confuse a Search Page with external services that search the entire Web or predefined areas of the Web.

If you plan to have your Web site development and production completed by an external production service, you may want to use the Search Page form twice. First, use it to communicate the search capability requirement to the production service to verify it is able to provide the interface at an acceptable price. Second, use it to form part of the Web site plan and submission package after the review/quotation process.

c. PAGE 3 OR 3+: FORM PAGE

An important feature of the Web is its ability to support bidirectional communications. This can be done by using interactive forms that may be customized to serve a wide variety of business needs such as soliciting customer feedback or making bookings or reservations.

With interactive forms, businesses can convey their messages, obtain timely client and prospect feedback, and support everything from electronic surveys to closing a sale. Even though generic e-mail facilities can be used, the convenience and efficiency of customized response forms and transaction initiators make using specialized interactive forms a requirement for most commercial sites.

Although customer response may not be immediate, the ability to receive a response in minutes or hours, as compared

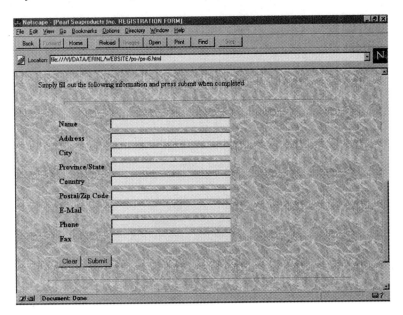

FIGURE #8
FORM PAGE

An easy-to-understand Form Page can be the source of orders for products via the Internet. Products or services are usually shown on Detail or Table Pages, but if there are only a few products available for order, the Form Page may include a brief summary of products.

to days or weeks for traditional mail services, makes this an efficient way to accelerate the sales/promotion process. Interactive forms require an HTML-based form, a forms-capable browser, and a script located on the server that will process and/or forward the information collected on the form to the appropriate facility or address. Again, you should make sure any external hosting service is able to process any interactive forms that you plan to include on your Web site.

d. PAGE 4 OR 4+: LINKS PAGE

Many sites include a Links Page where visitors are offered convenient links to preselected subjects or sites of interest. A link can be an image, word, title, or phrase that has been programmed to connect to related information that the Web site planner considers valuable. Links are usually provided for —

(a) sites with additional information on subjects related to the initial Web site;

(b) sites having unrelated but useful or interesting information for the site's target audience;

(c) sites having special facilities such as search facilities, weather sites, or mapping sites; and

(d) sites offering downloads of software, including latest browser versions and plug-ins.

The Links Page must be designed to reflect the needs of your individual Web site.

FIGURE #9
LINKS PAGE

This Web site uses a Links Page to point visitors to related sites, thank users for visiting the site, and encourage repeat visits.

40

6
DEVELOP YOUR WEB SITE PLAN: COMPLETING THE WEB SITE PLANNING MAP

Now that you have a better idea of the scope and direction of your business's Web site, you can begin to lay out the site itself. After deciding in general terms what content will go where, you are ready to design the infrastructure of the site.

This chapter discusses in detail how to plan the various page types in your site by using a Web Site Planning Map. You need to know which page types you want in your site before you will be able to fill in the Web Site Planning Map. Refer to the information in chapter 5 if you are not clear on what constitutes a certain page type.

Before you start mapping out your Web site, however, you also need to consider how your site will look.

a. DETERMINE WEB SITE STYLE

Now is the time to determine the look and feel of your site — its style. You will find three style sheets in section **b.** of Appendix 3. While each Web page may have a different background color, one style should be used for headers, navigation elements, and accents on all the pages to give your site continuity.

If you plan to use the Web site production service offered in Appendix 3, you should choose one of these three styles (you can view background selections at *www.sitestowin.com/BG*). If you plan to use a different production service or to produce your Web site yourself, these three style sheets will give you an idea of some of the styles available and the choices you need to make. You will want a style that best reflects the intent and focus of your Web site. The items you need to consider are:

(a) *The font style and size of all headers and subheaders to be included in the site.*

(b) *The type, size, color, and style of all accents to be used throughout the site.* These accents may be any graphic but are usually limited to lines or small accent pieces for simplicity.

(c) *The color and texture of backgrounds to be used in the Web site pages.* A site may include multiple background types, although a maximum of two to three different but complementary backgrounds is recommended for most small- to medium-sized Web sites. The backgrounds you select should be recorded by Web site page number. Include the name of the graphic file used to store the background.

b. USING THE WEB SITE PLANNING MAP

Once you have decided on a style, use the Web Site Planning Map (Worksheet #4) in Appendix 2 to create your own Web site map. The worksheet is composed of four sheets that are designed to be removed from the book and taped together, creating a map that is easy to use. Sample #4 shows an example of the map as completed for a fictitious Web site. You should refer to this as you map out the flow of your own Web site. The Web Site Planning Map is designed to visually communicate content, technical page types, and Web site organization.

At first glance, the Web Site Planning Map may look complicated. Be assured it is both logical and practical. The completed sample Web Site Planning Map is for a five-page Web site. The Map Worksheets can, of course, accommodate much larger sites — just copy additional blank Worksheets as necessary. As discussed in chapter 5 in broad terms, a typical five-page site usually consists of —

(a) Page 1: ID Page (or Combo Page)

(b) Page 2: Detail Page,

(c) Page 3: Table Page,

(d) Page 4: Form Page, and

(e) Page 5: Links Page.

However, you may want your site to be composed of an ID or Combo Page plus any combination of Detail Pages, Table Pages, Form Pages, and special purpose pages. Some of these types of pages, for example, a Table Page, might not be appropriate for your business. The Content Planner (Worksheet #3) you filled in while reading chapter 4 will help you determine which types of pages you should include.

Plan as many Web pages as you need. If your site will have more than five pages and you have used all the boxes of a certain page type on the map, use the optional pages to list your additional pages.

Since the page types have been explained in the previous chapter, you can begin filling out the Web Site Planning Map for your own Web site by following the step-by-step instructions in the sections below. If you wish to get an understanding of the larger picture, you may want to read all the way through this chapter before beginning the Web Site Planning Map Worksheet.

c. STANDARD PAGES

In chapter 7, you will construct the individual page types using detailed worksheets; with the Web Site Planning Map, you will do the groundwork for this process by recording the planning details for each page type. You may want to tear out and tape together your Web Site Planning Map Worksheet now in order to follow along with the map completion instructions.

1. ID Page

(a) **Page Number:** This reflects the page's placement in a logical sequence in the Web site. The ID Page or Combo Page will always be page one.

(b) **Image Name:** The name of the photo, logo, or illustration used in the ID Page.

(c) **File Name:** If the graphic is in a digital file, this is the computer file name.

(d) **Graphic Type:** Indicate whether the graphic is a photo, logo, or other graphic element.

(e) **Header Copy:** The text of the ID Page's header or title.

(f) **Detail Copy:** Optional text copy used in the ID Page summary statement (Ask your production house if there is a maximum number of lines or words available for this text.) Also note the name of the file if it is on a diskette.

(g) **Link Buttons:** This defines the page a link button is pointed to: link X goes to page X. Your site must have three pages or more to have link buttons.

(h) **Button Label:** The text for the navigation button.

(i) **Background:** The background color you have selected for this page.

SAMPLE #4
WEB SITE PLANNING MAP

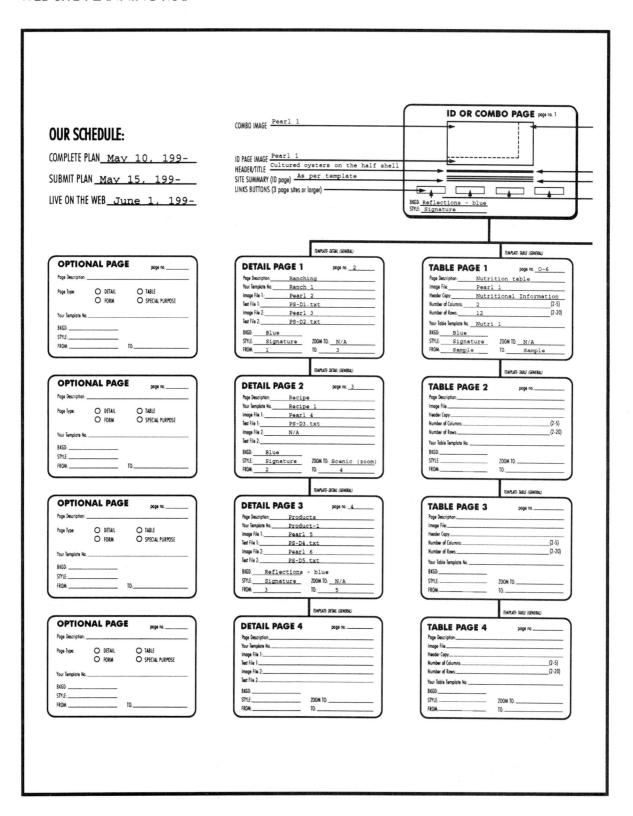

OUR SCHEDULE:

COMPLETE PLAN May 10, 199-

SUBMIT PLAN May 15, 199-

LIVE ON THE WEB June 1, 199-

COMBO IMAGE Pearl 1

ID OR COMBO PAGE page no. 1

ID PAGE IMAGE Pearl 1
HEADER/TITLE Cultured oysters on the half shell
SITE SUMMARY (ID page) As per template
LINKS BUTTONS (3 page sites or larger)

BKGD: Reflections - blue
STYLE: Signature

OPTIONAL PAGE page no. _____

Page Description: _____

Page Type: ○ DETAIL   ○ TABLE
            ○ FORM   ○ SPECIAL PURPOSE

Your Template No. _____

BKGD: _____
STYLE: _____
FROM: _____ TO: _____

TEMPLATE- DETAIL (GENERAL)

DETAIL PAGE 1 page no. _2_

Page Description: Ranching
Your Template No. Ranch 1
Image File 1: Pearl 2
Text File 1: PS-D1.txt
Image File 2: Pearl 3
Text File 2: PS-D2.txt

BKGD: Blue
STYLE: Signature ZOOM TO: N/A
FROM: 1 TO: 3

TEMPLATE- TABLE (GENERAL)

TABLE PAGE 1 page no. O-6

Page Description: Nutrition table
Image File: Pearl 1
Header Copy: Nutritional Information
Number of Columns: 2 (2-5)
Number of Rows: 12 (2-20)
Your Table Template No. Nutri 1
BKGD: Blue
STYLE: Signature ZOOM TO: N/A
FROM: Sample TO: Sample

OPTIONAL PAGE page no. _____

Page Description: _____

Page Type: ○ DETAIL   ○ TABLE
            ○ FORM   ○ SPECIAL PURPOSE

Your Template No. _____

BKGD: _____
STYLE: _____
FROM: _____ TO: _____

TEMPLATE- DETAIL (GENERAL)

DETAIL PAGE 2 page no. _3_

Page Description: Recipe
Your Template No. Recipe 1
Image File 1: Pearl 4
Text File 1: PS-D3.txt
Image File 2: N/A
Text File 2:

BKGD: Blue
STYLE: Signature ZOOM TO: Scenic (zoom)
FROM: 2 TO: 4

TEMPLATE- TABLE (GENERAL)

TABLE PAGE 2 page no. _____

Page Description: _____
Image File: _____
Header Copy: _____
Number of Columns: _____ (2-5)
Number of Rows: _____ (2-20)
Your Table Template No. _____
BKGD: _____
STYLE: _____ ZOOM TO: _____
FROM: _____ TO: _____

OPTIONAL PAGE page no. _____

Page Description: _____

Page Type: ○ DETAIL   ○ TABLE
            ○ FORM   ○ SPECIAL PURPOSE

Your Template No. _____

BKGD: _____
STYLE: _____
FROM: _____ TO: _____

TEMPLATE- DETAIL (GENERAL)

DETAIL PAGE 3 page no. _4_

Page Description: Products
Your Template No. Product-1
Image File 1: Pearl 5
Text File 1: PS-D4.txt
Image File 2: Pearl 6
Text File 2: PS-D5.txt

BKGD: Reflections - blue
STYLE: Signature ZOOM TO: N/A
FROM: 3 TO: 5

TEMPLATE- TABLE (GENERAL)

TABLE PAGE 3 page no. _____

Page Description: _____
Image File: _____
Header Copy: _____
Number of Columns: _____ (2-5)
Number of Rows: _____ (2-20)
Your Table Template No. _____
BKGD: _____
STYLE: _____ ZOOM TO: _____
FROM: _____ TO: _____

OPTIONAL PAGE page no. _____

Page Description: _____

Page Type: ○ DETAIL   ○ TABLE
            ○ FORM   ○ SPECIAL PURPOSE

Your Template No. _____

BKGD: _____
STYLE: _____
FROM: _____ TO: _____

TEMPLATE- DETAIL (GENERAL)

DETAIL PAGE 4 page no. _____

Page Description: _____
Your Template No. _____
Image File 1: _____
Text File 1: _____
Image File 2: _____
Text File 2: _____
BKGD: _____
STYLE: _____ ZOOM TO: _____
FROM: _____ TO: _____

TEMPLATE- TABLE (GENERAL)

TABLE PAGE 4 page no. _____

Page Description: _____
Image File: _____
Header Copy: _____
Number of Columns: _____ (2-5)
Number of Rows: _____ (2-20)
Your Table Template No. _____
BKGD: _____
STYLE: _____ ZOOM TO: _____
FROM: _____ TO: _____

IMAGE NAME: <u>PS logo</u>   FILE NAME: <u>Pearl 1</u>
○ PHOTO   ☒ LOGO   ○ GRAPHIC

HEADER/TITLE COPY: <u>Cultured oysters on the half shell</u>
DETAIL COPY - FILE NAME: <u>As per ID page template</u>

LINK BUTTONS (must be 3 page site or larger)
LINK 1 GOES TO PAGE <u>2</u>   BUTTON LABEL <u>Ranching</u>
LINK 2 GOES TO PAGE <u>3</u>   BUTTON LABEL <u>Recipes</u>
LINK 3 GOES TO PAGE <u>4</u>   BUTTON LABEL <u>Products</u>
LINK 4 GOES TO PAGE <u>5</u>   BUTTON LABEL <u>Ordering</u>

TEMPLATE- FORM (GENERAL)

FORM PAGE 1
page no. <u>5</u>

Form Description: <u>Order form</u>
Image File: <u>N/A</u>
Header Copy: <u>Foodservice buying instructions</u>
E-Mail Address: <u>pearlsea@sunshine.net</u>

Your Form Template No. <u>buying 1</u>

BKGD: <u>Reflections - blue</u>
STYLE: <u>Signature</u>   ZOOM TO: <u>N/A</u>
FROM: <u>4</u>   TO: <u>6</u>

TEMPLATE- SPECIAL PURPOSE

SPECIAL PURPOSE PAGE 1
page no. <u>6</u>

Page Description: *Links Page*

Image File: <u>Pearl 1</u>
Header Copy: <u>Try these aquaculture...</u>

Your Links Template No. <u>Links 1</u>

BKGD: <u>Blue</u>
STYLE: <u>Signature</u>
FROM: <u>5</u>   TO: <u>1</u>

TEMPLATE- FORM (GENERAL)

FORM PAGE 2
page no. _____

Form Description: _____
Image File: _____
Header Copy: _____
E-Mail Address: _____

Your Form Template No. _____

BKGD: _____
STYLE: _____   ZOOM TO: _____
FROM: _____   TO: _____

TEMPLATE- SPECIAL PURPOSE

SPECIAL PURPOSE PAGE 2
page no. <u>7</u>

Page Description: *Zoom Page*
Image File: <u>Pearl 4</u>
Header Copy: <u>The World is your Oyster...</u>
Text Copy (one line): <u>Contact info / e-mail</u>

Your Zoom Template No. <u>Zoom-1</u>
BKGD: <u>Blue</u>
STYLE: <u>Signature</u>
FROM: <u>3</u>   RETURN TO: <u>3</u>

TEMPLATE- FORM (GENERAL)

FORM PAGE 3
page no. _____

Form Description: _____
Image File: _____
Header Copy: _____
E-Mail Address: _____

Your Form Template No. _____

BKGD: _____
STYLE: _____   ZOOM TO: _____
FROM: _____   TO: _____

TEMPLATE- SPECIAL PURPOSE

SPECIAL PURPOSE PAGE 3
page no. <u>O-7</u>

Page Description: *Database Interface Page*

Will Be User Defined

Your DBI Template No. <u>DBI-1</u>
BKGD: <u>Blue</u>
STYLE: <u>Signature</u>
FROM: <u>Sample</u>   TO: <u>Sample</u>

TEMPLATE- FORM (GENERAL)

FORM PAGE 4
page no. _____

Form Description: _____
Image File: _____
Header Copy: _____
E-Mail Address: _____

Your Form Template No. _____

BKGD: _____
STYLE: _____   ZOOM TO: _____
FROM: _____   TO: _____

TEMPLATE- SPECIAL PURPOSE

SPECIAL PURPOSE PAGE 4
page no. <u>O-8</u>

Page Description: *Search Page*
Image File: <u>Pearl 1</u>
Header Copy: <u>Text Search Facility</u>
E-Mail Address: <u>pearlsea@sunshine.net</u>

Your Search Template No. <u>Search 1</u>

BKGD: <u>Reflections - blue</u>
STYLE: <u>Signature</u>
FROM: <u>Sample</u>   TO: <u>Sample</u>

FIGURE #10

MAP ID PAGE

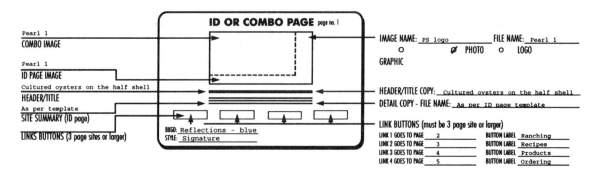

(j) **Style:** The style you have selected for all pages in the Web site.

2. Combo Page

(a) **Page Number:** This reflects the page's placement in a logical sequence in the Web site. The Combo Page or ID Page will always be page one.

(b) **Image Name:** The name of the photo, logo, or illustration used in the Combo Page.

(c) **File Name:** If the graphic is in a digital file, this is the computer file name.

(d) **Graphic Type:** Indicate whether the graphic is a photo, logo, or other graphic element.

(e) **Header Copy:** The text of the Combo Page's header or title.

(f) **Detail Copy:** The amount of copy should not cause the Combo Page to exceed normal page length. Also note the name of the file if it is on a diskette.

FIGURE #11

MAP COMBO PAGE

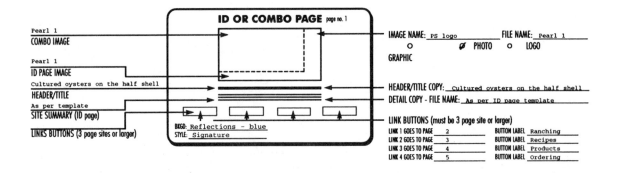

(g) **Link Buttons:** This defines the page a link button is pointed to: link X goes to page X. Your site must have three pages or more to have link buttons.

(h) **Button Label:** The text for the navigation button.

(i) **Background:** The background color you have selected for this page.

(j) **Style:** The style you have selected for all pages in the Web site.

3. Detail Page

(a) **Page Number:** This reflects the page's placement in a logical sequence in the Web site.

(b) **Page Description:** A brief description of the page and its contents.

(c) **Form Number:** The identification number you assign the worksheet and final form.

(d) **Image/File 1:** The image or file name (including digital) of the first major graphic/text on this page.

(e) **Text File 1:** The first text file for the page.

(f) **Image/Text File 2:** As above, but corresponding to the second major graphic/text on this page.

(g) **Background:** The background color you have selected for this page.

(h) **Style:** The style you have selected for all pages in the Web site.

(i) **Zoom To (optional):** Zoom Page description and number of page.

(j) **From:** The number of the Web site page linking to this page.

(k) **To:** The number of the next Web site page.

DETAIL PAGE 1 page no. 2

Page Description: Ranching

Your Template No. Ranch 1

Image File 1: Pearl 2

Text File 1: PS-D1.txt

Image File 2: Pearl 3

Text File 2: PS-D2.txt

BKGD: Blue

STYLE: Signature ZOOM TO: N/A

FROM: 1 TO: 3

FIGURE #12
MAP DETAIL PAGE

4. Table Page

(a) **Page Number:** This reflects the page's placement in a logical sequence in the Web site.

(b) **Page Description:** A brief description of the page and its contents.

(c) **Image/File:** Name of the image or digital image file for the major graphic on the Table Page.

(d) **Header Copy:** The text of the Table Page's header or title.

(e) **Number of Columns:** The number of columns required in the table.

(f) **Number of Rows:** The number of rows (cells) required for the information and for all titles, headers, and column labels.

(g) **Form Number:** The identification number you assign the worksheet and final form.

(h) **Background:** The background color you have selected for this page.

(i) **Style:** The style you have selected for all pages in the Web site.

(j) **Zoom To (optional):** Zoom Page description and page number.

(k) **From:** The number of the Web site page linking to this page.

(l) **To:** The number of the next Web site page.

FIGURE #13
MAP TABLE PAGE

TABLE PAGE 1 page no. _O-6_

Page Description:	Nutrition table
Image File:	Pearl 1
Header Copy:	Nutritional Information
Number of Columns:	2
Number of Rows:	12
Your Table Template No.	Nutri 1
BKGD:	Blue
STYLE: Signature	ZOOM TO: N/A
FROM: Sample	TO: Sample

5. Form Page

(a) **Page Number:** This reflects the page's placement in a logical sequence in the Web site.

(b) **Form Description:** A brief description of the form and its purpose.

(c) **Image/File:** Name of the image or digital image file for the major graphic on the Form Page.

(d) **Header Copy:** The text of the Form Page's header or title.

(e) **E-Mail Address:** E-mail address to which user can send the completed form.

(f) **Form Number:** The identification number you assign the worksheet and final form.

(g) **Background:** The background color you have selected for this page.

(h) **Style:** The style you have selected for all pages in the Web site.

(i) **Zoom To (optional):** Zoom Page description and page number.

(j) **From:** The number of the Web site page linking to this page.

(k) **To:** The number of the next Web site page.

FORM PAGE 1   page no.   5

Form Description: Order form
Image File: N/A
Header Copy: Foodservice buying instructions
E-Mail Address: pearlsea@sunshine.net

Your Form Template No.   buying 1

BKGD: Reflections - blue
STYLE: Signature   ZOOM TO: N/A
FROM: 4   TO: 6

FIGURE #14
MAP FORM PAGE

d. SPECIAL PURPOSE PAGES

As you will learn, special purpose pages go a step beyond basic display purposes within your Web site. They add interactive functions to your site and sometimes require special programming or information.

1. Links Page

(a) **Page Number:** This reflects the page's placement in a logical sequence in the Web site.

(b) **Page Description:** A brief description of the page and its contents.

(c) **Image/File:** Name of the image or digital image file for the major graphic on the Links Page.

(d) **Header Copy:** The text of the Links Page's header or title.

(e) **E-Mail Address (optional):** E-Mail address with which users can contact the person in your company responsible for the Web site.

(f) **Form Number:** The identification number you assign the worksheet and final form.

(g) **Background:** The background color you have selected for this page.

(h) **Style:** The style you have selected for all pages in the Web site.

(i) **From:** The number of the Web site page linking to this page.

(j) **To:** The number of the next Web site page.

FIGURE #15
MAP LINKS PAGE

SPECIAL PURPOSE PAGE 1

page no. 6

Page Description: *Links Page*

Image File: Pearl 1

Header Copy: Try these aquaculture...

Your Links Template No. Links 1

BKGD: Blue

STYLE: Signature

FROM: 5   TO: 1

2. Zoom Page

(a) **Page Number:** This reflects the page's placement in a logical sequence in the Web site.

(b) **Page Description:** A brief description of the page and its contents.

(c) **Image/File:** Name of the image or digital file to be used as the enlarged image on the Zoom Page.

(d) **Header Copy:** The text of the header or title of the Zoom Page.

(e) **Text Copy:** Text used as a label or caption to provide a description or other information about the Zoom image.

(f) **Form Number:** The identification number you assign the worksheet and final form.

(g) **Background:** The background color you have selected for this page.

(h) **Style:** The style you have selected for all pages in the Web site.

(i) **From:** The number of the Web site page linking to this page.

(j) **Return To:** The page number of the Web page to which the Zoom Page pertains.

SPECIAL PURPOSE PAGE 2

page no. _7_

Page Description: *Zoom Page*

Image File: _____ Pearl 4 _____

Header Copy: _____ The World is your Oyster... _

Text Copy (one line): ___ Contact info / e-mail _____

Your Zoom Template No. _Zoom-1_____

BKGD: __Blue____

STYLE: __Signature__

FROM: ___3____   RETURN TO: _3_

FIGURE #16
MAP ZOOM PAGE

3. Database Interface Page

(a) **Page Number:** This reflects the page's placement in a logical sequence in the Web site.

(b) **Page Description:** A brief description of the page and its contents.

(c) **Header Copy:** The text of the Database Interface Page's header or title.

(d) **Form Number:** The identification number you assign to the Database Interface worksheet and form.

(e) **Background:** The background color you have selected for this page.

(f) **Style:** The style you have selected for all pages in the Web site.

(g) **From:** The number of the Web site page linking to this page.

(h) **To:** The number of the next Web site page.

TIP:

Don't forget that one of the advantages of the Web is its potential for interaction. Be sure to incorporate interactive forms and e-mail links. Create a call for action and provide an easy way for users to answer that call.

FIGURE #17
MAP DATABASE
INTERFACE PAGE

SPECIAL PURPOSE PAGE 3

page no. ___O-7___

Page Description: *Database Interface Page*

Will Be User Defined

Your DBI Template No. ___DBI-1___

BKGD: ___Blue___

STYLE: ___Signature___

FROM: ___Sample___   TO: ___Sample___

4. Search Page

(a) **Page Number:** This reflects the page's placement in a logical sequence in the Web site.

(b) **Page Description:** A brief description of the page and its contents.

(c) **Image/File:** Name of the image or digital image file to be used as the enlarged image on the Search Page.

(d) **Header Copy:** The text of the Search Page's header or title.

(e) **E-Mail Address (optional):** E-Mail address with which users can contact the person in your company responsible for the Web site.

(f) **Form Number:** The identification number you assign to the Search worksheet.

(g) **Background:** The background color you have selected for this page.

(h) **Style:** The style you have selected for all pages in the Web site.

FIGURE #18
MAP SEARCH PAGE

SPECIAL PURPOSE PAGE 4

page no. ___O-8___

Page Description: *Search Page*

Image File: ___Pearl 1___

Header Copy: ___Text Search Facility___

E-Mail Address: ___pearlsea@sunshine.net___

Your Search Template No. ___Search 1___

BKGD: ___Reflections - blue___

STYLE: ___Signature___

FROM: ___Sample___   TO: ___Sample___

(i) **From:** The number of the Web site page linking to this page.

(j) **To:** The number of the next Web site page.

e. OPTIONAL PAGES

The optional pages don't have corresponding worksheets or forms at the back of the book, since they are only additional pages beyond the standard Web site size of five pages. An optional page may be any page type other than an ID or Combo Page (a site may contain only one ID or Combo Page). Make as many copies of worksheets for each type of Optional Page as you will need.

(a) **Page Number:** This reflects the page's placement in a logical sequence in the Web site.

(b) **Page Description:** A brief description of the page and its contents.

(c) **Page Type:** An optional page may be a Detail, Table, Form, or Special Purpose page.

(d) **Form Number/Background/Style/From/To:** See specific page type in sections **a.** and **b.** above.

7 LAYING OUT YOUR WEB PAGES

Before you begin completing the individual page type worksheets (found in Appendix 2), you should have laid out your content in a way that reflects the current Web site plan. It's a good idea to ask yourself: Does the plan continue to make sense? Does it flow properly? Does it communicate what you want it to in a way that will be understood and accepted by the target audience? Are there changes you can make that will increase the effectiveness of the content?

After you have assembled the content, begin completing the worksheets for each page type and ensure that your Web Site Planning Map and planners (Worksheets #1 to #4) reflect the latest information for your site. Don't forget about section **b.** of your Content Planner (Worksheet #3) — the text inventory record. It will provide you with a handy record of your text files and links, so use it!

You are now ready to begin working with the individual page design worksheets. You should draft your Web pages on the worksheets provided in Appendix 2. If you need more worksheets, photocopy the originals as required during your planning process. These worksheets, like the rest of the book, are covered by copyright, so reproduce only what is required during your planning process.

When you have reached a design that you are ready to use or submit for production, transfer the worksheet content to their corresponding forms — also in Appendix 2. These forms are designed to be easily torn out of the book, ready for you to use or submit to a production house for Web site production. These forms are also covered by copyright law, so the same rules apply as to the worksheets.

TIP:

It's a good idea to do a thorough search of the Web for sites published by companies in the same business as yours. They will have done some things that you will want to include on your site, and you will also see ways to distinguish your site from theirs.

Note: You should have completed the Site Preplanner (Worksheet #1) by this time. If you have not done so, complete it before proceeding.

The worksheets provide space for those who choose to type or print by hand the material to be input. These sheets (with the exception of the ID Page) are 8.5" x 11" — dimensions recognized in North America as a standard page size. See section **b.2.** in chapter 4 for a discussion of inputting text and how text is measured by most Web site production houses. Figure #2 in chapter 5 shows the amount of text that may be contained on a standard page.

When using the worksheets and final forms, you will see shaded areas for headers, table cells, graphic positioning, etc. You may either type or print in them, over them, or around them, depending on whether the box or line is applicable to your particular content for that page type. This is to allow you to organize your page copy in a way that makes sense to you, follows a general format, and can be understandable by any party that needs to review or work with it in the process of developing your Web site.

a. CREATING STANDARD PAGES

The following worksheet instructions provide a step-by-step explanation of the various types of page layouts commonly found in Web sites. Use these instructions as you complete the worksheets; they will save you time and spare you inconvenience later. Filled-in samples provide further explanation of how to complete the worksheets.

1. ID Page

Sample #5 shows a filled-in ID Page. The following steps will help you complete Worksheet #5 and its corresponding form.

(a) Assign the worksheet a unique identification or form number and enter this in the space provided at the lower left of the worksheet.

> **Note:** The form number refers to a unique identifier for the worksheet or final form; the page number refers to the page number that this page will occupy within the Web site.

(b) Enter the page number of this worksheet in the space provided for it on the lower right-hand corner of the worksheet.

(c) Print or type the image ID description and image file name in the shaded-in graphics/image box. Record the image information in the appropriate areas on the Content Planner and on your Web Site Planning Map.

(d) Enter copy for the page header or title in the next box down.

(e) Enter the descriptive text copy in the third box down. Copy may be limited by space — check with your production house before finalizing.

If you would like to prepare text on a separate page, type it or print it legibly. The text page should then be attached to the worksheet. If you prepare the text as an electronic file, attach a printed version to the worksheet and write the file name(s) on the worksheet in approximately the intended text position.

(f) Four rectangles are displayed at the bottom of the worksheet. These rectangles represent navigation elements which will allow viewers to conveniently go to specific sections or pages in your Web site.

You will probably not need all four elements, so you should leave unused elements blank (they will not appear on your ID Page). For each element you use, indicate on the worksheet which page the element should point to and write a one or two word description as a label for the section or page where the user will go. Record the navigation information in the appropriate area on your Web Site Planning Map.

(g) Using the space provided at the bottom of the worksheet, indicate if this Web page calls for any special requirements. These may include animation, 3-D effects, custom page backgrounds, database facilities, search engines, marquees, banners, traffic counters, or video and audio requirements. Special requirements necessitate additional communications between the client and the developer.

2. Combo Page

Sample #6 shows a filled-in Combo Page. It is designed to be a standard measure for your text input based on a 12-point font size and single spacing, as discussed in chapter 4, section **b.2.** To complete Worksheet #6 and its corresponding form:

(a) Assign the worksheet a unique form number and enter this in the space provided at the lower left of the worksheet.

(b) Enter the page number of this worksheet in the space provided for it on the lower right-hand corner of the worksheet.

PHOTO/LOGO/GRAPHIC
3.5" x 2"
IMAGE ID   PS Logo
IMAGE FILE NAME   Pearl 1

PLEASE INSERT YOUR PAGE HEADER/TITLE IN THE SPACE BELOW:

CULTURED OYSTERS ON THE HALF SHELL

PLEASE INSERT DESCRIPTIVE TEXT COPY IN THE SPACE BELOW:

SUMMARY: You can rely on Pearl Seaproducts for top quality oysters,
portion control, and consistent supply from the cold, pure waters
of British Columbia, Canada.

P.O. Box 1792, Sechelt, B.C., Canada V0N 3A0
Tel: (604) 740-0465   Fax: (604) 740-0467
pearlsea@sunshine.net

PLEASE INDICATE IN THE FOLLOWING BOXES WHERE YOU WISH THIS PAGE TO LINK:

PAGE NO. DESCRIPTION	2 Ranching	3 Recipes	4 Products	5 Ordering

FORM NO:_____Intro1_____ SPECIAL REQUIREMENT: ☐ YES ☒ NO   PAGE NO:_____1_____

(c) Enter copy for the page header or title.

(d) Print or type the image ID description and image file name in the shaded-in graphics/image box. Record the image information in the appropriate areas on the Content Planner and on your Web Site Planning Map.

(e) Enter the text copy below the graphics/image box or prepare text on a separate page in type or legible printing. Attach the text page to this worksheet (and eventually to the final version of the corresponding form). If you prepare the text as an electronic file, attach a printed version to the worksheet; the electronic file name(s) should be written on the worksheet in the intended text position.

(f) Fill in as many of the four rectangles at the bottom of the worksheet as you need. Indicate on the worksheet which page the element should point to and write a one- or two-word description as a label for the section or page where the user will go. Record the navigation information in the appropriate area on your Web Site Planning Map.

(g) Using the space provided at the bottom of the worksheet, indicate if this page will include any special requirements.

3. Detail Page

Sample #7 shows a filled-in Detail Page. The following steps will help you complete Worksheet #7 and its corresponding form.

(a) Enter the page number of this worksheet in the space provided for it on the lower right-hand corner of the worksheet. Also enter the form number on the lower left-hand corner of the worksheet.

(b) Enter the page header or title in the first box.

(c) Indicate placement of image(s) at the left, center, or right of the page. Keep your Detail Page to a maximum of two graphics/images. Also fill in the image ID and image file name lines. Record the image information in the appropriate areas on the Content Planner and on your Web Site Planning Map.

(d) Enter the text copy for the page in the blank space. Or, if you wish, text may be prepared on a separate page in type or legible printing. The text page should be attached to the worksheet. If you prepare the text as an electronic file, attach a printed version to the worksheet and write the file name(s) and names of images on the

PLEASE INSERT YOUR PAGE HEADER/TITLE IN THE BOX BELOW:

CULTURED OYSTERS ON THE HALF SHELL

PHOTO/LOGO/GRAPHIC
2.75" x 1.75"
IMAGE ID   PS Logo
IMAGE FILE NAME   Pearl 1

START CONTENT TYPE HERE:

Situated in remote and idyllic Jervis Inlet, British Columbia, and accessible only by boat and float plane, Pearl Seaproducts' three oyster ranches are among Canada's largest producers of live oysters on the half shell. Oysters grow well here, feeding naturally in the cold, pure waters. During the past ten years, Pearl Seaproducts has improved upon the culture of oysters with earth-friendly technology. Our oysters feed continuously in an ideal environment and grow more quickly than beach oysters. Harvested at a young age, our tray-cultured oysters are more tender and have a sweeter taste. You can rely on Pearl Seaproducts for top quality oysters, portion control, and consistent supply. Grown in trays, our oysters are easily monitored to ensure a ready inventory at all times. We have three varieties of live oysters available — in extra small, small, and medium sizes.

GRAPHIC   Right
IMAGE ID   Boxes
IMAGE FILE NAME   Pearl 3

With our scale of operations, Pearl guarantees a year-round supply of the world's finest oysters. Harvested weekly from the pristine waters of Canada's West Coast, our premium oysters are packed live and cup down in wet-lock boxes to retain their natural juices and extend shelf life. Pearl's oysters are inspected in a federally registered processing plant, insuring products which are safe, temperature controlled, and packed to the highest international standards. From our remote ranches on the Sunshine Coast, our oysters are delivered the same day to our distribution center in Vancouver for immediate shipment worldwide. Pearl's oysters will arrive at your place of business faster and fresher — in peak condition.

P.O. Box 1792, Sechelt, B.C., Canada V0N 3A0
Tel: (604) 740-0465   Fax: (604) 740-0467
pearlsea@sunshine.net

PLEASE INDICATE IN THE FOLLOWING BOXES WHERE YOU WISH THIS PAGE TO LINK:

PAGE NO. DESCRIPTION	2 Ranching	3 Recipes	4 Products	5 Ordering

FORM NO:_____Intro 1____ SPECIAL REQUIREMENT: ☐ YES ☒ NO   PAGE NO:_____1_____ worksheet in approximately the intended page position.

Note: Text may be entered directly over one or both of the watermarked image boxes if one or both boxes are not to be used for graphics placement.

(e) Enter the major page header as a separate entry on the worksheet. Text headers and subheaders should be placed as part of the body of text. Indicate headers and subheaders by bolding or underlining.

(f) Using the space provided at the bottom of the worksheet, indicate if this page will include any special requirements.

4. Table Page

Sample #8 shows a filled-in Table Page with a maximum of 5 columns and 12 rows. The table has been watermarked (faded) to allow you to enter text in the desired format. For example, if you need only 2 columns, each cell could be the width of 2.5 cell lengths, or if you require 4 columns, information could have a uniform width of 1.25 cell lengths. The cell with the most text determines the width and height of all cells in that column or row. To complete Worksheet #8 and its corresponding form:

(a) Assign the worksheet a unique form number and enter this in the space provided at the lower left-hand corner of the worksheet.

(b) Enter the page number of this worksheet in the space provided for it on the lower right-hand corner of the worksheet.

(c) Enter copy for the page header or title.

(d) (Optional) Indicate placement of image to the left, center, or right of page in shaded-in box. Fill in image ID description and image file name. Record the image information on the worksheet and in the appropriate areas in the Content Planner and on your Web Site Planning Map.

(e) Indicate the number of columns and rows that you want in the table. Enter the text copy for the page in a way that reflects the number of rows and columns. Underline or bold text that is to be used for cell headers or row and column labels.

Instead of entering the text directly on the worksheet, you might wish to prepare the text on a separate page in type or legible printing that clearly indicates the row and column configuration desired. If you do this, attach the text page to the worksheet. If you prepare the text

----

PLEASE INSERT YOUR PAGE HEADER/TITLE IN THE BOX BELOW:

OYSTER RANCHING - CULTURED OYSTERS ON THE HALF SHELL

2.75" x 1.75"
PLEASE SPECIFY ALIGNMENT BY PLACING AN "X" IN THE RELEVANT BOX
Left ☐   Right ☐   Center ☒
IMAGE ID   Trays
IMAGE FILE NAME   Pearl 2

START CONTENT TYPE HERE:

Situated in remote and idyllic Jervis Inlet, British Columbia, and accessible only by boat and float plane, Pearl Seaproducts' three oyster ranches are among Canada's largest producers of live oysters on the half shell. Oysters grow well here, feeding naturally in the cold pure waters. During the past ten years, Pearl Seaproducts has improved upon the culture of oysters with earth-friendly technology. Our oysters feed continuously in an ideal environment and grow more quickly than beach oysters. Harvested at a young age, our tray-cultured oysters are more tender and have a sweeter taste. You can rely on Pearl Seaproducts for top quality oysters, portion control, and consistent supply. Grown in trays, our oysters are easily monitored to ensure a ready inventory at all times. We have three varieties of live oysters available –- in extra small, small, and medium sizes.

2.75" x 1.75"
PLEASE SPECIFY ALIGNMENT BY PLACING AN "X" IN THE RELEVANT BOX
Left ☐   Right ☐   Center ☒
IMAGE ID   Boxes
IMAGE FILE NAME   Pearl 3

With our scale of operations, Pearl guarantees a year-round supply of the world's finest oysters. Harvested weekly from the pristine waters of Canada's West Coast, our premium oysters are packed live and cup down in wet-lock boxes to retain their natural juices and extend shelf life. Pearl's oysters are inspected in a federally registered processing plant, insuring products which are safe, temperature controlled, and packed to the highest international standards. From our remote ranches on the Sunshine Coast, our oysters are delivered the same day to our distribution center in Vancouver for immediate shipment worldwide. Pearl's oysters will arrive at your place of business faster and fresher — in peak condition.

FORM NO:_____Ranch 1___ SPECIAL REQUIREMENT: ☐ YES ☒ NO PAGE NO:_____2_____

PLEASE INSERT YOUR PAGE HEADER/TITLE IN THE BOX BELOW:

THE WORLD IS YOUR OYSTER AND OUR OYSTER IS FRESH AND PURE

2.75" x 1.75"
PLEASE SPECIFY ALIGNMENT BY PLACING AN "X" IN THE RELEVANT BOX
Left ☐ Right ☐ Center ☒
IMAGE ID   Scenic
IMAGE FILE NAME   Pearl 4

START CONTENT TYPE HERE:

There is a need for mother nature's wholesome foods in our busy lives, and our sweet, tender oysters are one of the most nutritionally complete foods. Feeding on natural plankton, they are high in Omega-3 fatty acids which protect against heart disease, arthritis, and other ailments. Oysters are also high in iron, an important element for a healthy lifestyle. And let's not forget their bounty of zinc, known to play an important role in the body's reproductive function. Just one more reason why we're passionate about our oysters!

Protein	9.4 g	Sodium	106 mg
Carbohydrate	5.0 g	Calcium	8 mg
Total Fat	2.3 g	Vitamin C	7%*
Saturated Fatty Acid	0.5 g	Iron	30%*
Omega-3 Fatty Acids	0.6 g	Zinc	60%*
Total Calories	70	*As % of daily recommended	
Cholesterol	36 mg	allowance	

NUTRITIONAL INFORMATION: per 100 g raw serving (approx. 4 oz.)

Enjoy our favorite recipes and send us your favorite:

"THE PURIST"
Pick the oyster shell up with your fingers, taking care not to spill the oyster liquor. Bring the broad end of the oyster to your lips, tip the shell and drink the juices, tilt your head back just slightly and, if necessary, nudge the oyster in with your fingertips. Taste the ocean!

CUCUMBER RELISH
1 medium Cucumber, peeled, seeded, and diced   1 tablespoon cider vinegar
1 tablespoon snipped fresh dill   1 tablespoon fresh lemon juice
Cracked black Pepper & Salt to taste   1 teaspoon dry sherry
Lemon wedges and fresh dill sprigs for garnish   Pinch cayenne pepper

Combine all ingredients. Refrigerate until ready to use.

*FORM NO:*____Recipe 1__*SPECIAL REQUIREMENT:* ☐ YES ☒ NO   *PAGE NO:*___3___

PLEASE INSERT YOUR PAGE HEADER/TITLE IN THE BOX BELOW:

A TASTE OF CULTURE

2.75" x 1.75"
PLEASE SPECIFY ALIGNMENT BY PLACING AN "X" IN THE RELEVANT BOX
Left ☐ Right ☐ Center ☒
IMAGE ID   PB Logo
IMAGE FILE NAME   Pearl 5

START CONTENT TYPE HERE:

Winner of the "People's Choice" award at the 1997 British Columbia
Wine and Oyster Festival in Vancouver, Pearl Bay is one of the West
Coast's top-selling half shell oysters. This tray-cultured oyster
has a mild, sweet taste with very tender meat; it is best served
raw with a twist of lemon. Pearl Bays are comfortable in a crowd
with a crisp Sauvignon Blanc and a dash of bravado.

Product Source: Canada
Species: Crassostrea gigas
Availability: Year Round
Sizes: Extra small 2" - 2 1/2" -
                    Small 2 1/2" - 3 1/4" - Medium 3 1/4" - 4 1/4"

These tray-cultured oysters have a beautiful shell with a very deep
cup and a high meat-to-shell ratio.

GRAPHIC   Left
IMAGE ID   SI Logo
IMAGE FILE NAME   Pearl 6

Our Summer Ice Oyster is a specialty product, available only from
May through August. New tray-culture methods ensure this oyster
retains its winter condition. The meat is firm and sweet, with a
hint of summer fresh cucumber. These morsels are an exquisite
experience in the shade of a beach umbrella as you raise a glass of
Chardonnay to the oyster, to the day.

Product Source: Canada
Species: Crassostrea gigas
Availability: May through August
Sizes: Extra small 2" - 2 1/2" - Small 2 1/2" - 3 1/4"
These tray-cultured oysters have a beautiful shell with a very deep
cup and a high meat-to-shell ratio.

Storage: Live oysters should be refrigerated at
                    35-40°F (2-4°C)
Shelf life: 2 weeks under properly chilled conditions.

FORM NO: _____ Product 1 SPECIAL REQUIREMENT: ☐ YES ☒ NO   PAGE NO: __4__ as an electronic file, attach a printed version to the corresponding worksheet and write the file name(s) on the worksheet in the intended cell position.

(f) Using the space provided at the bottom of the worksheet, indicate if this page will include any special requirements.

5. Form Page

Sample #9 shows a filled-in Form Page; it is designed to facilitate the placement of both standard and user-defined form elements. To complete Worksheet #9 and its corresponding form:

(a) Assign the worksheet a unique form number and enter this in the space provided at the lower left-hand corner of the worksheet.

(b) Enter the page number of this worksheet in the space provided for it on the lower right-hand corner of the worksheet.

(c) Enter copy for the page header or title in the first box.

(d) Record the Form Page information in the appropriate areas on the Worksheet, the Content Planner, and on your Web Site Planning Map.

(e) Indicate information, questions, or comments which will be attached to the optional form element shown on the worksheet. (This is represented by the second rectangle from the bottom of the Form Page.)

(f) Enter the e-mail address to which the form is to be directed in the space provided for it on the bottom of the worksheet.

(g) Using the space provided at the bottom of the worksheet, indicate if this page will include any special requirements.

b. CREATING SPECIAL PURPOSE PAGES

We've now covered, in detail, the standard pages found in most Web sites. In this section, we will look at special purpose pages — the pages that add functionality to your site. As you now know, the most common special purpose pages are Links Pages, Zoom Pages, Database Interface Pages, and Search Pages.

1. Links Page

To prepare a Links Page, you will need to fill in Worksheet #10 (and its corresponding form). Refer to Sample #10, which shows a completed Links Page worksheet.

SAMPLE #8
TABLE PAGE

PLEASE INSERT YOUR PAGE HEADER/TITLE IN THE BOX BELOW:

NUTRITIONAL INFORMATION per 100 g raw serving (approx. 4 oz.)

2.75" x 1.75"
PLEASE SPECIFY ALIGNMENT BY PLACING AN "X" IN THE RELEVANT BOX
Left ❑ *Right* ❑ *Center* ☒
IMAGE ID　　　　　　　　　PS Logo
IMAGE FILE NAME　　　　　Pearl 1

NUMBER OF COLUMNS:　2

NUMBER OF ROWS:　12

Protein	9.4 g		
Carbohydrate	5.0 g		
Total Fat	2.3 g		
Saturated Fatty Acid	0.5 g		
Omega-3 Fatty Acids	0.6 g		
Total Calories	70		
Cholesterol	36 mg		
Sodium	106 mg		
Calcium	8 mg		
Vitamin C	*7%		
Iron	*30%		
Zinc	*60%		

*As % of daily recommended allowance

P.O. Box 1792 Sechelt, B.C., Canada V0N 3A0
Tel: (604) 740-0465　Fax: (604) 740-0467
pearlsea@sunshine.net

PLEASE INDICATE IN THE FOLLOWING BOXES WHERE YOU WISH THIS PAGE TO LINK:

PAGE NO.	2	3	4	5
DESCRIPTION	Ranching	Recipes	Products	Ordering

FORM NO:　Nutri 1　*SPECIAL REQUIREMENT:* ❑ YES ☒ NO　*PAGE NO:*　5

SAMPLE #9
FORM PAGE

PLEASE INSERT YOUR PAGE HEADER/TITLE IN THE BOX BELOW:

FOOD SERVICE BUYING INSTRUCTIONS

INSTRUCTIONS TO USERS

NAME: George Seagull
STREET: 2323 Rockedge Place
CITY: Pleasantville
STATE/PROVINCE: Stateston
ZIP/POSTAL CODE: 45678
PHONE: (200) 333-4444
FAX: (200) 333-4454
E-MAIL ADDRESS: gseagull@rocky.net

IS THIS A ☒ HOME ADDRESS ❑ COMPANY ADDRESS
IF COMPANY, PLEASE PROVIDE COMPANY NAME: _____

PLEASE USE THE FOLLOWING TEXT AREA FOR ANY COMMENTS, INQUIRIES OR SUGGESTIONS THAT
YOU MAY HAVE REGARDING YOUR WEB SITE AND ITS CONTENT:

For more product information, contact Pearl Seaproducts Inc. at the
above address or simply fill in the information form above.

In California & Washington contact:
Marinelli Shellfish, Space L17 Pier 33, San Francisco, CA 94111
Tel: (415) 391-0846
FAX: (415) 391-0850

In Vancouver, Victoria, Kelowna contact:
Albion Fisheries Ltd., 1077 Great Northern Way, Vancouver, B.C. V5T 1E1
Tel: (604) 875-0166
FAX: (604) 875-0644

In the U.S.A./Southeast Asia/Europe/Canada contact:
Pearl Seaproducts Inc.
E-mail: pearlsea@sunshine.net

FORM NO:_____ Buying 1 _SPECIAL REQUIREMENT: ❑ YES ☒ NO   PAGE NO: ___6___

(a) Assign the worksheet a unique form number and enter this in the space provided at the lower left-hand corner of the page.

(b) Enter the page number of this worksheet in the space provided on the lower right-hand corner of the page.

(c) Enter copy for the page header or title in the box at the top of the page.

(d) Record the image ID and file name information in the shaded-in box and in the appropriate areas on the Content Planner and the Web Site Planning Map.

(e) Enter the copy for a category header (if required) in the next box down.

(f) Complete the links area of the worksheet by providing detailed link information in the following format: Site Description-Site Address

(g) (Optional) Insert the e-mail address of the person to be contacted if users experience difficulties with any of these links or when link-oriented information is to be exchanged.

(h) Using the boxes provided on the bottom of the page, or by clearly marking the worksheet, indicate how the site visitor is to return to other pages within the site. You may choose to simply provide a "back" button which would return the visitor to a previous selection page, or you may choose to provide buttons that would take the visitor to a particular content or section page. If nothing is entered, the Web site developer will provide what he or she considers the most efficient method of navigation for the visitor.

(i) Using the space provided at the bottom of the worksheet, indicate if this page will include any special requirements.

2. Zoom Page

Sample #11 and the steps below will help you fill out Worksheet #11 and its corresponding form.

(a) Assign a unique form number to the worksheet and enter this in the space provided on the lower left-hand corner of the page.

(b) Enter the page number of this worksheet in the space provided for it on the lower right-hand corner of the page.

(c) Enter copy for the page header or title.

PLEASE INSERT YOUR PAGE HEADER/TITLE IN THE BOX BELOW:

THANKS FOR VISITING, PLEASE COME AGAIN

2.75" x 1.75"
PLEASE NOTE THAT THIS GRAPHIC IS OPTIONAL.
PLEASE SPECIFY ALIGNMENT BY PLACING AN "X" IN THE RELEVANT BOX
Left ☐ *Right* ☐ *Center* ☒
IMAGE ID   PS Logo
IMAGE FILE NAME   Pearl 1

PLEASE INSERT YOUR CATEGORY HEADER IN THE BOX BELOW: (note category headers are optional)

TRY THESE AQUACULTURE/SEAFOOD LINKS

PLEASE INSERT NAMES AND URL ADDRESSES OF UP TO 20 SITES YOU WISH TO POINT TO IN THE
SPACE BELOW:

```
Shellfish recipes -
    http://www.ichef.com/recipes.html
Marine Species Database -
    http.//www.mbl.edu/html/mrc/specimens.html
World Aquaculture Society -
    http://www.ansc.purdue.edu/aquanic/was.html
Aquaculture Association of Canada -
    http://dragger.ifmt.nf.ca/mi/aac/
National Shell fisheries Association -
    http://www.shellfish.org/
Northern Aquaculture Magazine -
    http://www.naqua.com/
Aquanet -
    http://www.aquanet.com/

         P.O. Box 1792, Sechelt, B.C., Canada V0N 3A0
           Tel: (604) 740-0465  Fax: (604) 740-0467
                E-mail to pearl@fleethouse.com
```

PLEASE INDICATE IN THE FOLLOWING BOXES WHERE YOU WISH THIS PAGE TO LINK:

| PAGE NO. | ID Page 1 | | | |
| DESCRIPTION | Home | | | |

*FORM NO:*____Links 1____ *SPECIAL REQUIREMENT:* ☐ YES ☐ NO   *PAGE NO:* _7_

(d) Record the image information on the shaded image area, the Content Planner, and the Web Site Planning Map.

(e) Enter any copy which should accompany the expanded image when displayed in the shaded area.

(f) Using the space that is available in the box below the header copy, insert a brief note explaining where the expanded image is linked (i.e., Link zoom to image "Scenic" from page 3).

(g) Using the space provided at the bottom of the page, indicate if this Web page will include any special requirements.

3. Database Interface Page

Database Interface Pages require that there be an integrated database in your Web site; you will need additional integrated services. Worksheet #12 (and its corresponding form) focuses on the information required for an external review and/or quotation. See Sample #12 for an example of a completed Database Interface Page worksheet.

(a) Assign the worksheet a unique form number and enter this in the space provided at the lower left-hand corner of the page.

(b) Enter the page number of this worksheet in the space provided for it on the lower right-hand corner of the page.

(c) Enter copy for the page header or title in the first box.

(d) Record the image information in the shaded image area, on the Content Planner, and on the Web Site Planning Map.

(e) Enter any copy which should accompany the request for quotation in the space under the shaded area. This copy is usually used to explain to visitors to your Web site how a query may be entered into the database facility. A sample description is suggested.

The enquiry area is likely to be unique to your particular database and may only be finalized after the database design has been completed. Sample information is included.

(f) Designing and creating a database is not a casual task and may only be accomplished successfully if the client and the developer have communicated effectively during the planning and design process. This process is always to be considered a special requirement within a Web site.

SAMPLE #11
ZOOM PAGE

Pearl Seaproducts Inc.
P.O. Box 1792 Sechelt, B.C., Canada V0N 3A0
Tel: (604) 740-0465 Fax: (604) 740-0467
E-mail to pearlsea@sunshine.net

PLEASE INSERT YOUR PAGE HEADER/TITLE IN THE BOX BELOW:

ON-LINE OYSTER GUIDE

2.75" x 1.75"
PLEASE NOTE THAT THIS GRAPHIC IS OPTIONAL
PLEASE SPECIFY ALIGNMENT BY PLACING AN "X" IN THE RELEVANT BOX
Left ☐ *Right* ☐ *Center* ☒
IMAGE ID   PS Logo
IMAGE FILE NAME   Pearl 1

HEADER OR COPY TO BE INSERTED HERE:

Pearl Seaproducts is pleased to provide a comprehensive on-line information resource for those desiring more information about oyster varieties from around the world. You may select information using any of the following criteria:

Geographic Source: country(ies) where variety may be found
Variety: common variety name
Size: large, medium, small
Preparation: cooked, raw
Price: high, medium, economy
Availability: enter month of requirement

ENQUIRY AREA

Geographic Source: Canada
Variety: Pearl Bay
Size: medium
Preparation: raw
Price: high
Availability: July

REQUIRES
QUOTATION

Pearl Seaproducts Inc.
P.O. Box 1792 Sechelt, B.C., Canada V0N 3A0
Tel: (604) 740-0465 Fax: (604) 740-0467
pearlsea@sunshine.net

PLEASE INDICATE IN THE FOLLOWING BOXES WHERE YOU WISH THIS PAGE TO LINK:

PAGE NO. DESCRIPTION	2 Ranching	3 Recipes	4 Products	5 Ordering

FORM NO: __DBI 1__   SPECIAL REQUIREMENT: YES - *This page requires integrated database* PAGE NO: __9__

4. Search Page

The Search Page is used only when an integrated search facility has been developed to enable a text search of the Web site content. Sample #13 will give you some guidance for filling in Worksheet #13 and its corresponding form.

(a) Assign the worksheet a unique form number and enter this in the space provided on the lower left-hand corner of the page.

(b) Enter the page number of this worksheet in the space provided for it on the lower right-hand corner of the page.

(c) Enter copy for the page header or title.

(d) Record the image information in the shaded image area, on the Content Planner, and on the Web Site Planning Map.

(e) Enter any copy which should accompany the Search Page in the space below the shaded area. This copy is usually used for an explanation of how a search may be initiated. It is probably best to use a brief sample or keyword description.

   Note: The keyword area may be unique to your particular search environment and may only be finalized after the search facility has been completed.

(f) Use the space under the search request to briefly outline the requirements of your search facility. This may serve as a starting point in the design process for the search facility.

(g) A search facility is always to be considered a special requirement within a Web site. Using the space provided at the bottom of the worksheet, indicate that this page has a special requirement.

PLEASE INSERT YOUR PAGE HEADER/TITLE IN THE BOX BELOW:

TEXT SEARCH FACILITY

2.75" x 1.75"
PLEASE NOTE THAT THIS GRAPHIC IS OPTIONAL
PLEASE SPECIFY ALIGNMENT BY PLACING AN "X" IN THE RELEVANT BOX
Left ☐   Right ☐   Center ☒
IMAGE ID   PS Logo
IMAGE FILE NAME   Pearl 1

PLEASE INSERT A BRIEF DESCRIPTION OF WHAT THIS PAGE IS USED FOR IN THE SPACE BELOW:

This search facility is a utility for locating information which is contained within the Pearl Seaproducts Web site. Enter a word or a series of words in the keyword window below.

Sample Keywords: Oyster Festival

SEARCH REQUEST DESCRIPTION

The search facility required within this Web site is to be limited to a simple text search linked to a single keyword or series of keywords.

PLEASE INDICATE IN THE FOLLOWING BOXES WHERE YOU WISH THIS PAGE TO LINK:

PAGE NO.	2	3	4	5
DESCRIPTION	Ranching	Recipes	Products	Ordering

FORM NO: ___Search 1___   SPECIAL REQUIREMENT: YES - This page requires integrated search engine
PAGE NO: ____10____

8 TAKING THE TIME TO REVIEW

Congratulations! You have now completed the planning process for your Web site. Through your efforts, your company has likely saved significant dollars in this critical phase while acquiring a Web site plan that is professional and effective.

Now that the planning is complete, review the process that you and your team have gone through. Are you satisfied with the results? Have all stakeholders been given an opportunity for review and feedback? If you were starting the process now, what would you change to improve the process or results? How can you use this process to review and update your ongoing Web facility?

Take the time to review the information that you originally entered in the Site Preplanner. Is it still accurate? Have you created a site that will meet your objectives?

How does the budget look? Are the figures that you originally used for Worksheet #2 following instructions found in chapter 3 still accurate? Has management agreed to these numbers and approved funding and resource allocation for the first year?

Review chapter 3 on your Web site production options. You are now ready to decide how you want to technically develop your Web site. Do you want to do it yourself, making use of your own skills and those of your staff, or do you want to use an external production house?

You also need to consider promotion of your Web site. How will you do it and do you need it? How can you optimize promotion both on and off the Web? Turn to chapter 9 to begin developing your promotional strategies.

TIP:

Remember . . . focus on the message you want to communicate to your target audience.

9
PROMOTING YOUR WEB SITE

The World Wide Web has achieved phenomenal acceptance and growth over its short, meteoric life. Today there are estimated to be between 50 million and 70 million pages of information accessible through this medium, and the rate of growth continues to accelerate. The real challenge facing an organization establishing a Web site now and in the future, will be to produce a site capable of fighting its way to virtual daylight. Making a site visible and keeping it visible in this deluge of information requires serious commitment.

Promoting your Web site is a task that requires organization, discipline, and tenacity. Promoting your Web site should occur both on and off the Internet.

a. PROMOTING YOUR WEB SITE OFF THE INTERNET

A successful Web site is usually created to supplement or complement existing activities or facilities of an organization. The relationship between the Web site and these elements should be symbiotic from the beginning. As soon as you have decided to create a Web site and have confirmed your Web address, let the world and, more importantly, your staff, customers, and potential clients know what you are about to do. Print the Web site address on all business publications. This includes:

- Annual reports and other regular reporting publications
- Brochures, catalogs, and guides
- Internal and external newsletters

As well, print the Web site address in all advertising materials regardless of medium. This includes:

- Fax transmissions
- Company business cards, letterhead, and envelopes
- Promotional materials, media releases, and give-aways
- Signage
- Uniforms and corporate ID clothing

b. PROMOTING YOUR WEB SITE ON THE INTERNET

1. Search engines

Your Web site needs to be listed in the growing number of search engines to ensure it is seen by potential clients or consumers. These search engines make your site visible and accessible to the Internet community, and visibility and accessibility are key ingredients in a successful site.

What are search engines and how do they work in Web site promotion? Search engines gather information about Web sites by accepting registrations and/or by using devices such as robots, spiders, and Webcrawlers to index sites. Keywords for your site are stored in the search engines' databases. When a Web surfer types keywords into a particular search engine, those keywords are compared to the keywords taken by the spider or from the registration information. The search engine then displays addresses of sites corresponding to the search criteria. The surfer can click on your address to be taken immediately to your site.

Search engines check their databases for information based on these keywords. Because there are usually numerous Web sites with matching or similar keywords, the search engine displays a selectable number of Web sites in the order of how closely each matches the search criteria. For example, a search engine may display the ten most relevant Web sites and then allow the user to view the next ten matching Web sites and so on, until the user has found what he or she is looking for or the list is exhausted. Most users prefer to find a result in the first ten Web sites rather than searching further through the list. The closer your keywords match those found in the top ten, the closer you are to having your Web site noticed.

There are numerous search facilities, each with its own strengths, weaknesses, and areas of specialization. All search facilities host Web site information databases, although they vary in size, data collection, search and selection criteria, and efficiency.

2. Selecting keywords

What keywords can get your Web site noticed? The answer to this question is crucial to the promotion of your Web site. Spend some time thinking about the key words used to describe your organization and its products or services. The following questions will help you determine keywords for your Web site:

- What three words come to mind when you think about your company and its products or services?

- What other words or phrases do you hear or use regularly in discussion of these subjects?

- What industries or business groups would your organization or its products or services be generally identified with?

- What words, phrases, labels, categories, etc., are applicable to your competitors, clients, and targeted prospects?

- What geographic keywords do you think are important?

Now that you have a list of potential keywords, prioritize them by importance or estimated effectiveness. If possible, look at the Web sites of your competitors. What keywords do your competitors use? How do yours compare? If yours are different, it is not an indication that yours are wrong but rather that you view business differently or that you have taken greater care in your selection.

Once you have developed your list of keywords, spend some time submitting these keywords to the various search engines and indexes. Chances are it will take several weeks and many attempts to get your keywords registered with all of the search engines and indexes you have chosen. Keep checking regularly (about every ten days) to see if your site comes up when you search with your keywords. If it doesn't, resubmit your keywords and check again in ten days. If your keyword submission has been processed, pay attention to the results to determine the effectiveness of your keywords. For example, is your site 1,000 in a list of 1,200 Web sites matching a particular keyword? As a result of experience gained over several weeks and on several search facilities, you will refine and fine-tune your keywords.

3. Site summary statements

Keywords are not the only way to promote your site on-line. It is also a good idea to have a brief summary statement on the first page of the site (this statement may be designed to be invisible to site visitors). The summary statement is usually inserted by site developers unless it is already provided by the client. Search engines will search the terms used in the statement, and your statement will show up as as "advertisement" for your site in the list of sites found under a particular keyword.

You can create keywords or submission summaries when the site is planned or anytime afterward during the promotional process. You should write two concise summary statements for your Web site. One summary should be no longer than 25 words and should contain as many of the priority keywords as possible. The other summary should be a one-line description of the site.

There are several registration services available on the Internet that will register your Web site with multiple search engines. These services, when they work, represent an invaluable tool to promote your site. But these registration services also receive overwhelming traffic and may give no guarantee or confirmation that your site has been registered.

The best method is to individually register your site. The registration process often takes anywhere from six weeks to two months.

4. Page titles

Another key to visibility is the insertion of a descriptive page title on all of your pages. This title may be a source of information for automated Web search facilities.

c. INTERNET JUNK MAIL

How do you directly inform potentially interested parties of your presence via the Internet? If you are a regular Internet e-mail user, you may have already received junk mail sent to you over the Internet. Chances are you didn't appreciate it, and if it happened on a regular basis you would probably become pretty vocal about your displeasure. Junk mail is anything that Web users receive unsolicited from parties that broadcast or send volume mail to individuals with little regard to applicability or interest. Do not participate in this activity.

If you want to let interested parties know of your existence, try the following:

(a) Identify which audiences or groups really will benefit from your Web site.

(b) Determine the existence of interest groups or discussion groups on the Internet catering to the identified audiences.

(c) Write a very brief invitation to view your new or revised site with the Web address and, at most, your 25-word description of the site.

(d) Where possible, contact the moderator or group administrator to obtain permission or assistance to post the invitation to the relevant interest or discussion groups.

(e) If the group is unmoderated, submit the invitation. Do not resubmit unless the site undergoes revision or significant expansion.

(f) Be very sensitive to any negative reaction. Realize that information is valued by those interested in a given topic. What is of value to one audience may be junk mail to another audience. Take care to genuinely qualify your audience and keep your message brief, factual, and unobtrusive.

Usenet, a large discussion group connected to the Internet, can also be a useful way to inform people of your Web site. Often you can announce — but not advertise — your site to the various discussion groups.

TIP:

Add the plural to each of your keywords. Search engines often find their results in the plural not the singular!

10 WEB SITE UPDATES AND MAINTENANCE

Once your site is fully operational, you still need to update content and keep the site operating properly. Any changes in products, services, prices, or other information about your business that would be of benefit to your customers should be updated as soon as possible. Part of the responsibility of maintaining this important information tool is to schedule regular reviews of its content and operation.

Because your Web site relies on a myriad of computer technologies to deliver its message to the world, there is a possibility that something in the programming of the site itself, or in any of the computer technologies that help deliver it, could malfunction. For these reasons, as well as because of advances in Web site technology that might be of significant benefit to your business, you need to monitor both the operation of your Web site and any pertinent advances in Internet technology. Keep these factors in mind, and your investment of time and money will pay off for years to come.

1
APPENDIX
PREPLANNING
WORKSHEETS

WORKSHEET #1
SITE PREPLANNER

What will this site be focused on, and how is this focus expected to change in the future?

❏ Our organization ❏ Our product(s) ❏ An event or specific promotion

Detail: _____

_____

_____

_____

What is our primary objective in creating this site?

❏ Promotion ❏ Generating sales ❏ Education service/support

Detail: _____

_____

_____

_____

What message should the site deliver and who is the audience? _____

_____

_____

_____

Are there existing messages and/or established images that must be incorporated in the Web site? Detail: _____

_____

_____

_____

Is there a critical launch date? ❏ Yes ❏ No

Detail: _____

_____

_____

_____

What is the anticipated/required launch date? _____

_____

_____

_____

_____

How will we define and quantify success or failure?

Success: _____

_____

_____

_____

Failure: _____

_____

_____

_____

Who will have responsibility for maintaining the site? _____

_____

_____

_____

_____

Planning/Design

Option A — In-house Planning Activities

Resource Material $_____

<u>Staff Cost_____</u> based upon____ staff participation hours

Option A Total $_____

-or-

Option B — External Planning Services

External Resource Fee $_____

<u>Staff Cost_____</u> based upon____ staff participation hours

Option B Total $_____

Development/Production

Option A — In-house Site Production

Resource Materials $_____

<u>Staff Cost_____</u> based upon____ staff participation hours

Option A Total $_____

-or-

Option B — External Site Production

Production Fee $_____

<u>Staff Cost_____</u> based upon____ staff participation hours

Option B Total $_____

Hosting

Option A — Internal Web Site Hosting

Hardware Costs $_____/mo.

Software Costs   _____/mo.

Telecommunications Costs   _____/mo.

Staff Costs   _____/mo.

<u>Other Costs_____</u>/mo.

Option A Total $_____/mo.

-or-

Option B — External Web Site Hosting

Hosting Fee	$_____	based upon a monthly fee of $_____
Staff Cost	_____	based upon ____ staff participation hours
Option B Total	$_____	

On-line Promotion

You should plan on spending a minimum of 15 hours to on-line promotion of your Web site within the first six weeks of operation. This is only a suggested minimum. The success of your Web site is dependent upon both the quality and visibility of the site. The more hours spent efficiently promoting your Web site should result in greater visibility on the Web and within your targeted audience.

Option A — Promotional Costs — In-house Resources

Promotion $ _____ based upon____ staff hrs. of promotion at $____/hr.

-or-

Option B — Promotional Costs — External Resources

Promotion $ _____ based upon____ hrs. of promotion at $_____/hr.

Other Promotion

Production and placement of promotional banners within commercial sites $ _____

Use of commercial listing services $_____

Direct cost of additional advertising of the Web site in other media $ _____

Content Updates

For budgeting purposes, estimate the approximate number of hours per month required to facilitate basic content changes. The first step is to determine what content is subject to change and how often that change is likely to occur. If changes are limited to simple text changes, the time required to perform the updates to the Web site is approximately 1.5 times the period required to make a textual change within a word processing document. This allows for resource time required to make the change and upload the changes to the server.

Estimated monthly resource hours for updates _____

Estimated monthly cost of updates based upon_____resource hours

at $ _____ /hour = $_____

Maintenance

Web site maintenance refers to the cost associated with keeping your Web site current with the general level of quality and sophistication found within Web sites of similar size and focus. The technologies and techniques associated with Web site development and management are rapidly changing, resulting in the rapid dating of Web sites that do not change with these new facilities. You should review and renew your Web site at least once a year. If your site stays approximately the same size and does not require the introduction of additional technology services, the cost associated with maintaining the site on an annual basis, at a level consistent with the general state of the Web, is estimated to be approximately 30% of the original design and production costs. This percentage may be higher for very small sites and lower for larger sites.

Estimated maintenance cost based upon the above information $ _____

First Year Web Site Budget

	In-house	External
Planning/Design Costs	$_____	$_____
Development Production Costs	_____	_____
Hosting Fees	_____	_____
On-line Promotion Fees	_____	_____
Other Promotional Fees	_____	_____
Content Updating Fees	_____	_____
Maintenance Fees	_____	_____

Total first year Web site cost $ _____ + $ _____ = $ _____

WORKSHEET #3
CONTENT PLANNER

<u>SECTION A</u> Preliminary planning meeting

Date: _____

Attendees: _____

_____

Primary person/team: _____

Target deadline for receiving images and text:_____

Web site type: _____

Web site size (number of input pages): _____

Page types to be included (see chapter 5):

_____

_____

_____

_____

_____

_____

_____

_____

_____

Photos/images required

	Description	Page no.	Source	Date req'd	Date rec'd	✗
1.						❏
2.						❏
3.						❏
4.						❏
5.						❏
6.						❏
7.						❏
8.						❏
9.						❏
10.						❏

Text/copy required

Description	Page no.	Source	Date req'd	Date rec'd	X
1. _____					☐
2. _____					☐
3. _____					☐
4. _____					☐
5. _____					☐
6. _____					☐
7. _____					☐
8. _____					☐
9. _____					☐
10. _____					☐

Fill in the following if applicable:

Date package sent to production company:_____ via: ☐ mail ☐ courier

Anticipated site completion date: _____

SECTION B Text inventory record

Page 1	Page type: _____	File name:_____
Page 2	Page type: _____	File name:_____
Page 3	Page type: _____	File name:_____
Page 4	Page type: _____	File name:_____
Page 5	Page type: _____	File name:_____
Page 6	Page type: _____	File name:_____
Page 7	Page type: _____	File name:_____
Link page 1	Linked from page: _____	Link word/phrase: _____
Link page 2	Linked from page: _____	Link word/phrase: _____
Link page 3	Linked from page:_____	Link word/phrase: _____
Link page 4	Linked from page: _____	Link word/phrase: _____
Link page 5	Linked from page: _____	Link word/phrase: _____
Link page 6	Linked from page: _____	Link word/phrase: _____
Link page 7	Linked from page: _____	Link word/phrase: _____
Link page 8	Linked from page: _____	Link word/phrase: _____

2 APPENDIX
WEB SITE
PLANNING MAP:
map pages,
worksheets,
and forms

WORKSHEET #4
WEB SITE PLANNING MAP

Pages 105 to 111 contain the Web Site Planning Map. The map has been printed in a large format and split into four sections to make it easy to use. Carefully remove the pages from the book. Then attach the pages as indicated in the diagram below using the dotted lines as a guide. Now you are ready to fill in the map.

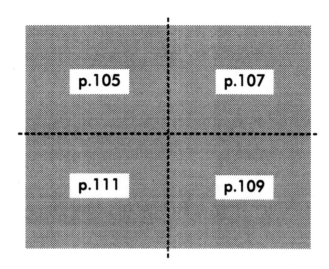

Web Site Planning Map

OUR SCHEDULE:

COMPLETE PLAN _____

SUBMIT PLAN _____

LIVE ON THE WEB _____

COMBO IMAGE _____

ID PAGE IMAGE _____
HEADER/TITLE _____
SITE SUMMARY (ID page) _____
LINKS BUTTONS (3 page sites or larger) _____

BKGD:
STYLE:

OPTIONAL PAGE
page no. _____

Page Description: _____

Page Type:
○ DETAIL   ○ TABLE
○ FORM   ○ SPECIAL PURPOSE

Your Template No. _____

BKGD: _____
STYLE: _____
FROM: _____   TO: _____

OPTIONAL PAGE
page no. _____

Page Description: _____

Page Type:
○ DETAIL   ○ TABLE
○ FORM   ○ SPECIAL PURPOSE

Your Template No. _____

TEMPLATE- DETAIL (GENERAL)

DETAIL PAGE 1
page no. _____

Page Description: _____

Your Template No. _____

Image File 1: _____
Text File 1: _____
Image File 2: _____
Text File 2: _____

BKGD: _____
STYLE: _____   ZOOM TO: _____
FROM: _____   TO: _____

TEMPLATE- DETAIL (GENERAL)

DETAIL PAGE 2
page no. _____

Page Description: _____

Your Template No. _____

Image File 1: _____
Text File 1: _____
Image File 2: _____
Text File 2: _____

TEMPLATE- TABL   pag

TABLE PAGE 1

Page Description: _____
Image File: _____
Header Copy: _____
Number of Columns: _____
Number of Rows: _____

Your Table Template No. _____

BKGD: _____
STYLE: _____   ZOOM TO: _____
FROM: _____   TO: _____

TEMPLATE- TABL   pag

TABLE PAGE 2

Page Description: _____
Image File: _____
Header Copy: _____
Number of Columns: _____
Number of Rows: _____

Your Table Template No. _____

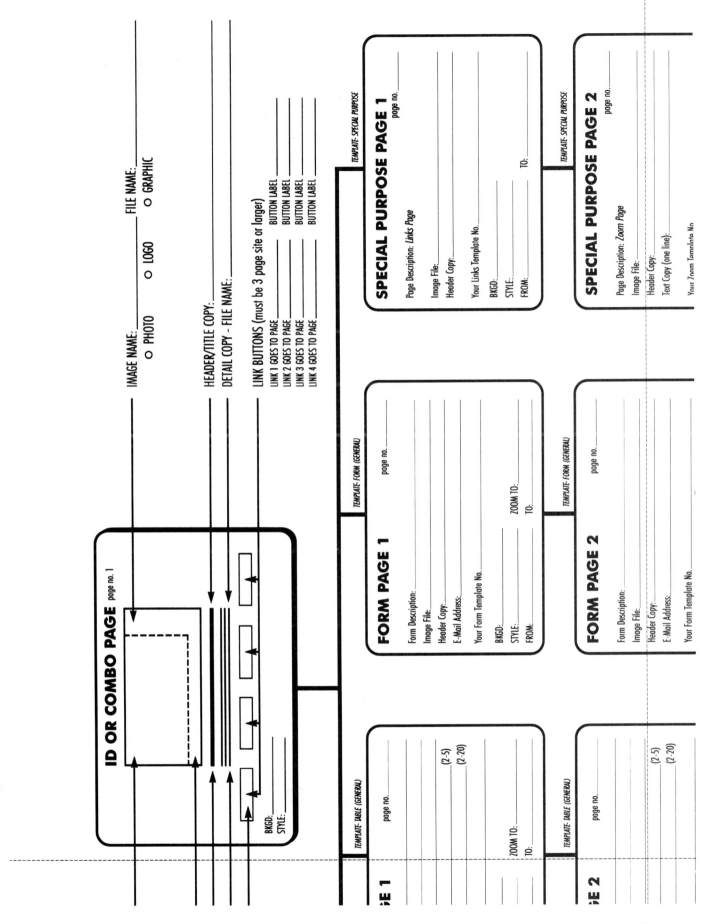

ID OR COMBO PAGE page no. 1

IMAGE NAME: _____ FILE NAME: _____
○ PHOTO   ○ LOGO   ○ GRAPHIC

HEADER/TITLE COPY: _____
DETAIL COPY - FILE NAME: _____

LINK BUTTONS (must be 3 page site or larger)
LINK 1 GOES TO PAGE _____ BUTTON LABEL
LINK 2 GOES TO PAGE _____ BUTTON LABEL
LINK 3 GOES TO PAGE _____ BUTTON LABEL
LINK 4 GOES TO PAGE _____ BUTTON LABEL

BKGD: _____
STYLE: _____

TEMPLATE: TABLE (GENERAL)

TEMPLATE: FORM (GENERAL)

FORM PAGE 1 page no. _____

Form Description: _____
Image File: _____
Header Copy: _____
E-Mail Address: _____
Your Form Template No. _____

BKGD: _____   ZOOM TO: _____
STYLE: _____   TO: _____
FROM: _____

TEMPLATE: FORM (GENERAL)

FORM PAGE 2 page no. _____

Form Description: _____
Image File: _____
Header Copy: _____
E-Mail Address: _____
Your Form Template No. _____

TEMPLATE: SPECIAL PURPOSE

SPECIAL PURPOSE PAGE 1 page no. _____

Page Description: *Links Page*

Image File: _____
Header Copy: _____

Your Links Template No. _____

BKGD: _____
STYLE: _____
FROM: _____   TO: _____

TEMPLATE: SPECIAL PURPOSE

SPECIAL PURPOSE PAGE 2 page no. _____

Page Description: *Zoom Page*
Image File: _____
Header Copy: _____
Text Copy (one line): _____
Your Zoom Template No.

TEMPLATE: TABLE (GENERAL)

GE 1 page no. _____

(2-5)
(2-20)

ZOOM TO: _____
TO: _____

GE 2 page no. _____

(2-5)
(2-20)

Page Description: *Zoom Page*
Image File: _____
Header Copy: _____
Text Copy (one line): _____
Your Zoom Template No. _____
BKGD: _____
STYLE: _____
FROM: _____
RETURN TO: _____

TEMPLATE- SPECIAL PURPOSE

SPECIAL PURPOSE PAGE 3

page no. _____

Page Description: *Database Interface Page*

Will Be User Defined

Your DBI Template No. _____
BKGD: _____
STYLE: _____
FROM: _____
TO: _____

TEMPLATE- SPECIAL PURPOSE

SPECIAL PURPOSE PAGE 4

page no. _____

Page Description: *Search Page*
Image File: _____
Header Copy: _____
E-Mail Address: _____
Your Search Template No. _____
BKGD: _____
STYLE: _____
FROM: _____
TO: _____

Form Description: _____
Image File: _____
Header Copy: _____
E-Mail Address: _____
Your Form Template No. _____
BKGD: _____
STYLE: _____
FROM: _____
ZOOM TO: _____
TO: _____

TEMPLATE- FORM (GENERAL)

FORM PAGE 3

page no. _____

Form Description: _____
Image File: _____
Header Copy: _____
E-Mail Address: _____
Your Form Template No. _____
BKGD: _____
STYLE: _____
FROM: _____
ZOOM TO: _____
TO: _____

TEMPLATE- FORM (GENERAL)

FORM PAGE 4

page no. _____

Form Description: _____
Image File: _____
Header Copy: _____
E-Mail Address: _____
Your Form Template No. _____
BKGD: _____
STYLE: _____
FROM: _____
ZOOM TO: _____
TO: _____

(2-5) _____
(2-20) _____
ZOOM TO: _____
TO: _____

TEMPLATE- TABLE (GENERAL)

GE 3

page no. _____

(2-5) _____
(2-20) _____
ZOOM TO: _____
TO: _____

TEMPLATE- TABLE (GENERAL)

GE 4

page no. _____

(2-5) _____
(2-20) _____
ZOOM TO: _____
TO: _____

TABLE PAGE (TEMPLATE: TABLE)

Page Description: ___
Image File: ___
Header Copy: ___
Number of Columns: ___
Number of Rows: ___
Your Table Template No. ___
BKGD: ___
STYLE: ___
FROM: ___
ZOOM TO: ___
TO: ___
page ___

TABLE PAGE 3 (TEMPLATE: TABLE)

Page Description: ___
Image File: ___
Header Copy: ___
Number of Columns: ___
Number of Rows: ___
Your Table Template No. ___
BKGD: ___
STYLE: ___
FROM: ___
ZOOM TO: ___
TO: ___
page ___

TABLE PAGE 4

Page Description: ___
Image File: ___
Header Copy: ___
Number of Columns: ___
Number of Rows: ___
Your Table Template No. ___
BKGD: ___
STYLE: ___
FROM: ___
ZOOM TO: ___
TO: ___

DETAIL PAGE (TEMPLATE: DETAIL (GENERAL))

Page Description: ___
Your Template No. ___
Image File 1: ___
Text File 1: ___
Image File 2: ___
Text File 2: ___
BKGD: ___
STYLE: ___
FROM: ___
ZOOM TO: ___
TO: ___
page no. ___

DETAIL PAGE 3 (TEMPLATE: DETAIL (GENERAL))

Page Description: ___
Your Template No. ___
Image File 1: ___
Text File 1: ___
Image File 2: ___
Text File 2: ___
BKGD: ___
STYLE: ___
FROM: ___
ZOOM TO: ___
TO: ___
page no. ___

DETAIL PAGE 4

Page Description: ___
Your Template No. ___
Image File 1: ___
Text File 1: ___
Image File 2: ___
Text File 2: ___
BKGD: ___
STYLE: ___
FROM: ___
ZOOM TO: ___
TO: ___

OPTIONAL PAGE

Page Description: ___
Page Type: ○ DETAIL   ○ TABLE
            ○ FORM   ○ SPECIAL PURPOSE
Your Template No. ___
BKGD: ___
STYLE: ___
FROM: ___
TO: ___
page no. ___

OPTIONAL PAGE

Page Description: ___
Page Type: ○ DETAIL   ○ TABLE
            ○ FORM   ○ SPECIAL PURPOSE
Your Template No. ___
BKGD: ___
STYLE: ___
FROM: ___
TO: ___
page no. ___

OPTIONAL PAGE

Page Description: ___
Page Type: ○ DETAIL   ○ TABLE
            ○ FORM   ○ SPECIAL PURPOSE
Your Template No. ___
BKGD: ___
STYLE: ___
FROM: ___
TO: ___
page no. ___

WORKSHEET #5
ID PAGE

PHOTO/LOGO/GRAPHIC
3.5" x 2"
IMAGE ID
IMAGE FILE NAME

PLEASE INSERT YOUR PAGE HEADER/TITLE IN THE SPACE BELOW:

PLEASE INSERT DESCRIPTIVE TEXT COPY IN THE SPACE BELOW:

PLEASE INDICATE IN THE FOLLOWING BOXES WHERE YOU WISH THIS PAGE TO LINK:

PAGE NO. DESCRIPTION			

FORM NO:_____ SPECIAL REQUIREMENT: ❏ YES ❏ NO PAGE NO:_____

ID PAGE

PHOTO/LOGO/GRAPHIC
3.5" x 2"
IMAGE ID
IMAGE FILE NAME

PLEASE INSERT YOUR PAGE HEADER/TITLE IN THE SPACE BELOW:

PLEASE INSERT DESCRIPTIVE TEXT COPY IN THE SPACE BELOW:

PLEASE INDICATE IN THE FOLLOWING BOXES WHERE YOU WISH THIS PAGE TO LINK:

PAGE NO. DESCRIPTION				

FORM NO:_____ SPECIAL REQUIREMENT: ❑ *YES* ❑ *NO* *PAGE NO:_____*

WORKSHEET #6
COMBO PAGE

PLEASE INSERT YOUR PAGE HEADER/TITLE IN THE BOX BELOW:

PHOTO/LOGO/GRAPHIC
2.75" x 1.75"
IMAGE ID
IMAGE FILE NAME

START CONTENT TYPE HERE:

PLEASE INDICATE IN THE FOLLOWING BOXES WHERE YOU WISH THIS PAGE TO LINK:

PAGE NO. DESCRIPTION			

FORM NO:_____ SPECIAL REQUIREMENT: ❏ YES ❏ NO   PAGE NO:_____

COMBO PAGE

PLEASE INSERT YOUR PAGE HEADER/TITLE IN THE BOX BELOW:

PHOTO/LOGO/GRAPHIC
2.75" x 1.75"
IMAGE ID
IMAGE FILE NAME

START CONTENT TYPE HERE:

PLEASE INDICATE IN THE FOLLOWING BOXES WHERE YOU WISH THIS PAGE TO LINK:

PAGE NO.
DESCRIPTION

FORM NO:_____ SPECIAL REQUIREMENT: ❑ YES ❑ NO   PAGE NO:_____

WORKSHEET #7
DETAIL PAGE

PLEASE INSERT YOUR PAGE HEADER/TITLE IN THE BOX BELOW:

2.75" x 1.75"
PLEASE SPECIFY ALIGNMENT BY PLACING AN "X" IN THE RELEVANT BOX
Left ❑   Right ❑   Center ❑
IMAGE ID
IMAGE FILE NAME

START CONTENT TYPE HERE:

FORM NO:_____SPECIAL REQUIREMENT: ❑ YES ❑ NO PAGE NO: _____

DETAIL PAGE

PLEASE INSERT YOUR PAGE HEADER/TITLE IN THE BOX BELOW:

2.75" x 1.75"
PLEASE SPECIFY ALIGNMENT BY PLACING AN "X" IN THE RELEVANT BOX
Left ❑ Right ❑ Center ❑
IMAGE ID
IMAGE FILE NAME

START CONTENT TYPE HERE:

FORM NO:_____SPECIAL REQUIREMENT: ❑ YES ❑ NO PAGE NO: _____

WORKSHEET #8
TABLE PAGE

PLEASE INSERT YOUR PAGE HEADER/TITLE IN THE BOX BELOW:

2.75" x 1.75"
PLEASE SPECIFY ALIGNMENT BY PLACING AN "X" IN THE RELEVANT BOX
Left ❑ *Right* ❑ *Center* ❑
IMAGE ID
IMAGE FILE NAME

NUMBER OF COLUMNS:

NUMBER OF ROWS:

PLEASE INDICATE IN THE FOLLOWING BOXES WHERE YOU WISH THIS PAGE TO LINK:

PAGE NO. DESCRIPTION			

FORM NO:_____SPECIAL REQUIREMENT: ❑ YES ❑ NO   PAGE NO: _____

TABLE PAGE

_____

PLEASE INSERT YOUR PAGE HEADER/TITLE IN THE BOX BELOW:

2.75" x 1.75"
PLEASE SPECIFY ALIGNMENT BY PLACING AN "X" IN THE RELEVANT BOX
Left ☐   Right ☐   Center ☐
IMAGE ID
IMAGE FILE NAME

NUMBER OF COLUMNS:
NUMBER OF ROWS:

_____

PLEASE INDICATE IN THE FOLLOWING BOXES WHERE YOU WISH THIS PAGE TO LINK:

PAGE NO. DESCRIPTION				

FORM NO:_____SPECIAL REQUIREMENT: ☐ YES ☐ NO   PAGE NO: _____

WORKSHEET #9
FORM PAGE

PLEASE INSERT YOUR PAGE HEADER/TITLE IN THE BOX BELOW:

INSTRUCTIONS TO USERS

      NAME:
      STREET:
      CITY:
      STATE/PROVINCE:
      ZIP/POSTAL CODE:
      PHONE:
      FAX:
      E-MAIL ADDRESS:

IS THIS A   ❑   HOME ADDRESS   ❑   COMPANY ADDRESS
IF COMPANY, PLEASE PROVIDE COMPANY NAME: _____

PLEASE USE THE FOLLOWING TEXT AREA FOR ANY COMMENTS, INQUIRIES OR SUGGESTIONS THAT YOU MAY HAVE REGARDING YOUR WEB SITE AND ITS CONTENT:

FORM NO:_____SPECIAL REQUIREMENT: ❑ YES ❑ NO   PAGE NO: _____

FORM PAGE

PLEASE INSERT YOUR PAGE HEADER/TITLE IN THE BOX BELOW:

INSTRUCTIONS TO USERS

NAME:

STREET:

CITY:

STATE/PROVINCE:

ZIP/POSTAL CODE:

PHONE:

FAX:

E-MAIL ADDRESS:

IS THIS A ❑ HOME ADDRESS ❑ COMPANY ADDRESS

IF COMPANY, PLEASE PROVIDE COMPANY NAME: _____

PLEASE USE THE FOLLOWING TEXT AREA FOR ANY COMMENTS, INQUIRIES OR SUGGESTIONS THAT YOU MAY HAVE REGARDING YOUR WEB SITE AND ITS CONTENT:

FORM NO:_____SPECIAL REQUIREMENT: ❑ YES ❑ NO   PAGE NO: _____

WORKSHEET #10
LINKS PAGE

PLEASE INSERT YOUR PAGE HEADER/TITLE IN THE BOX BELOW:

2.75" x 1.75"
PLEASE NOTE THAT THIS GRAPHIC IS OPTIONAL.
PLEASE SPECIFY ALIGNMENT BY PLACING AN "X" IN THE RELEVANT BOX
Left ❑ Right ❑ Center ❑
IMAGE ID
IMAGE FILE NAME

PLEASE INSERT YOUR CATEGORY HEADER IN THE BOX BELOW: (note category headers are optional)

PLEASE INSERT NAMES AND URL ADDRESSES OF UP TO 20 SITES YOU WISH TO POINT TO IN THE SPACE BELOW:

PLEASE INDICATE IN THE FOLLOWING BOXES WHERE YOU WISH THIS PAGE TO LINK:

PAGE NO. DESCRIPTION				

FORM NO:_____SPECIAL REQUIREMENT: ❑ YES ❑ NO   PAGE NO: _____

LINKS PAGE

PLEASE INSERT YOUR PAGE HEADER/TITLE IN THE BOX BELOW:

2.75" x 1.75"
PLEASE NOTE THAT THIS GRAPHIC IS OPTIONAL.
PLEASE SPECIFY ALIGNMENT BY PLACING AN "X" IN THE RELEVANT BOX
Left ☐ *Right* ☐ *Center* ☐
IMAGE ID
IMAGE FILE NAME

PLEASE INSERT YOUR CATEGORY HEADER IN THE BOX BELOW: (note category headers are optional)

PLEASE INSERT NAMES AND URL ADDRESSES OF UP TO 20 SITES YOU WISH TO POINT TO IN THE SPACE BELOW:

PLEASE INDICATE IN THE FOLLOWING BOXES WHERE YOU WISH THIS PAGE TO LINK:

PAGE NO. DESCRIPTION				

FORM NO:_____SPECIAL REQUIREMENT: ☐ *YES* ☐ *NO*   *PAGE NO: _____*

PLEASE INSERT YOUR PAGE HEADER/TITLE IN THE BOX BELOW:

ENLARGED IMAGE
5.5" X 3.25"
PLEASE SPECIFY ALIGNMENT BY PLACING AN "X" IN THE RELEVANT BOX
Left ❑ *Right* ❑ *Center* ❑
IMAGE ID
IMAGE FILE NAME

PLEASE INDICATE IN THE FOLLOWING BOXES WHERE YOU WISH THIS PAGE TO LINK:

PAGE NO. DESCRIPTION			

FORM NO:_____ SPECIAL REQUIREMENT: ❑ YES ❑ NO   PAGE NO: _____

ZOOM PAGE

PLEASE INSERT YOUR PAGE HEADER/TITLE IN THE BOX BELOW:

ENLARGED IMAGE
5.5" X 3.25"
PLEASE SPECIFY ALIGNMENT BY PLACING AN "X" IN THE RELEVANT BOX
Left ☐ *Right* ☐ *Center* ☐
IMAGE ID
IMAGE FILE NAME

PLEASE INDICATE IN THE FOLLOWING BOXES WHERE YOU WISH THIS PAGE TO LINK:

PAGE NO. DESCRIPTION			

FORM NO:_____SPECIAL REQUIREMENT: ☐ YES ☐ NO   PAGE NO: _____

WORKSHEET #12
DATABASE INTERFACE PAGE

PLEASE INSERT YOUR PAGE HEADER/TITLE IN THE BOX BELOW:

2.75" x 1.75"
PLEASE NOTE THAT THIS GRAPHIC IS OPTIONAL
PLEASE SPECIFY ALIGNMENT BY PLACING AN "X" IN THE RELEVANT BOX
Left ❏   Right ❏   Center ❏
IMAGE ID
IMAGE FILE NAME

HEADER OR COPY TO BE INSERTED HERE:

ENQUIRY AREA

REQUIRES
QUOTATION

PLEASE INDICATE IN THE FOLLOWING BOXES WHERE YOU WISH THIS PAGE TO LINK:

PAGE NO. DESCRIPTION				

FORM NO:_____SPECIAL REQUIREMENT: ❏ YES ❏ NO   PAGE NO: _____

141

DATABASE INTERFACE PAGE

PLEASE INSERT YOUR PAGE HEADER/TITLE IN THE BOX BELOW:

2.75" x 1.75"
PLEASE NOTE THAT THIS GRAPHIC IS OPTIONAL
PLEASE SPECIFY ALIGNMENT BY PLACING AN "X" IN THE RELEVANT BOX
Left ☐ Right ☐ Center ☐
IMAGE ID
IMAGE FILE NAME

HEADER OR COPY TO BE INSERTED HERE:

ENQUIRY AREA

REQUIRES
QUOTATION

PLEASE INDICATE IN THE FOLLOWING BOXES WHERE YOU WISH THIS PAGE TO LINK:

PAGE NO. DESCRIPTION				

FORM NO:_____SPECIAL REQUIREMENT: ☐ YES ☐ NO   PAGE NO: _____

WORKSHEET #13
SEARCH PAGE

PLEASE INSERT YOUR PAGE HEADER/TITLE IN THE BOX BELOW:

2.75" x 1.75"
PLEASE NOTE THAT THIS GRAPHIC IS OPTIONAL
PLEASE SPECIFY ALIGNMENT BY PLACING AN "X" IN THE RELEVANT BOX
Left ❏ *Right* ❏ *Center* ❏
IMAGE ID
IMAGE FILE NAME

PLEASE INSERT A BRIEF DESCRIPTION OF WHAT THIS PAGE IS USED FOR IN THE SPACE BELOW:

SEARCH REQUEST DESCRIPTION

PLEASE INDICATE IN THE FOLLOWING BOXES WHERE YOU WISH THIS PAGE TO LINK:

PAGE NO. DESCRIPTION				

*FORM NO:*_____ *SPECIAL REQUIREMENT:* ❏ *YES* ❏ *NO*   *PAGE NO:* _____

SEARCH PAGE

PLEASE INSERT YOUR PAGE HEADER/TITLE IN THE BOX BELOW:

2.75" x 1.75"
PLEASE NOTE THAT THIS GRAPHIC IS OPTIONAL
PLEASE SPECIFY ALIGNMENT BY PLACING AN "X" IN THE RELEVANT BOX
Left ❑ *Right* ❑ *Center* ❑
IMAGE ID
IMAGE FILE NAME

PLEASE INSERT A BRIEF DESCRIPTION OF WHAT THIS PAGE IS USED FOR IN THE SPACE BELOW:

SEARCH REQUEST DESCRIPTION

PLEASE INDICATE IN THE FOLLOWING BOXES WHERE YOU WISH THIS PAGE TO LINK:

PAGE NO. DESCRIPTION			

FORM NO:_____SPECIAL REQUIREMENT: ❑ YES ❑ NO   PAGE NO: _____

3
APPENDIX
FLEET HOUSE
PRODUCTION SERVICES

a. RECEIVE A REBATE FOR THE RETAIL PURCHASE PRICE OF THIS BOOK

Winning Web Sites has been written to help you plan and design your Web site. This book contains all the samples, worksheets, and information you need to complete the planning and design stages of developing your Web site. Once you are ready to actually produce your site, you have the choice of doing it yourself or choosing to use a professional Web site services company.

The Web site service company on whose processes and experience *Winning Web Sites* has been based is Fleet House Information Management Solutions Inc. If you decide to use Fleet House to produce your Web site,

---

you will be credited with a rebate*
deductible from the cost of Fleet House services.
This rebate will be equivalent
to the retail purchase price
of this Self-Counsel book
Winning Web Sites.

In order to qualify for this rebate, you will need to submit a completed Fleet House Order Form within 90 days of your purchase of *Winning Web Sites.* You will also need to provide a cash register tape or similar proof-of-purchase of the book.

Self-Counsel Press does not necessarily endorse, nor accept any responsibility for, your use of the services of Fleet House Information Management Services Inc. The purpose of this option is to provide you with a straightforward application of the planning and design work that you have conducted in this book. Any relationship that you choose to enter into with Fleet House Management Information Services Inc. will be a two party relationship without any real or implied relationship with Self-Counsel Press or any of its affiliated companies.

If you wish to pursue this option, please read the following submission procedure.

* Void where prohibited by law

b. FLEET HOUSE PRODUCTION SERVICES

a. Fleet House HQLC (high quality low cost) submission procedure

The Web site production services of Fleet House Information Management Solutions Inc. are referred to as HQLC (High Quality, Low Cost) production services. HQLC production services are designed to work efficiently with the plan you have created by following this book. Fleet House will ensure that you receive the highest possible production quality at the lowest cost to you.

In order for your submission to be complete and to avoid unnecessary delays, you will need to:

(a) copy the final information on the worksheets to the corresponding blank forms at the back of the book, ensuring that all information is clear and complete;

(b) ensure that any required text files or hard copy text pages accompany the submitted forms;

(c) ensure that all graphics are clearly labeled (the label should be affixed to the back or other adjacent area, not on the image to be scanned) with ID, page, and position information to ensure proper placement; and

(d) ensure that your submission contents are properly packaged for shipment. You may send the contents by mail, UPS, or by a service of your choice. Regardless of the means of shipment, ensure that you are not sending originals or "only copies."

When using Fleet House production services, we ask that you:

- do not send any oversized hard copy documents larger than 8.5" x 14";

- do not send slides or transparencies as they cannot be accommodated without delay and extra cost; and

- do not send originals or "only copies."

It is important to remember that Fleet House charges by input page rather than by output length. (There is one exception: the graphic-rich ID Page tends to be designed to fit one screen length for user convenience and visual impact.)

b. Style Sheets

You have three appearance options available if you choose to use Fleet House to produce your Web site. These are shown in Sample #14. Select a style that best reflects the intent and focus of your Web site. The style sheet can also be previewed in color on the Web at *www.sitestowin.com/style*. You will be able to see the different colors from which you can choose at this Web site.

1. Classic

The classic style features a serif font for all heading graphics and a classic selection of lines and accents. The navigational facilities feature either a traditional block button or a standard hypertext link.

2. Contemporary

The contemporary style features a sans serif font for all heading graphics and a contemporary selection of lines and accents. The navigational facilities feature either circular or block configuration buttons that have been stylized and integrated with directional text.

3. Signature

The signature style features a choice of either serif or sans serif heading graphics. Lines and accents are coordinated to provide a pleasing visual impact. The navigational facilities feature either a three-dimensional spherical look or the use of stylized text (matching your choice of serif or sans serif heading graphics).

All styles offer a wide range of textured and solid colored backgrounds that may be used within the individual pages.

It is important to note that while a Web site may include only one style, it can incorporate several backgrounds. Backgrounds within the site may be selected on a page-by-page basis. Usually the number of backgrounds contained in a small- to medium-sized site is limited to one or two. This is a matter of personal preference, so feel free to select the background(s) as you see fit. Please document your choices on the bottom of the style sheets.

Classic Web Site Style Sheet

Headings: Times New Roman

Accents: (Please "x" the desired accent for your site.)

Lines: ○ **Marble**   ————————   ○ **Standard line embossed**

○ **Precious Metal**   ————————   Line color utilized will be co-ordinated with background color and texture selected.

Navigational Elements:

○   Text   ○ HyperText

Option 1: features a defined graphical button   Option 2: this option features a text based trigger

Backgrounds:

Concrete

blue   tan   white

Mist

blue   red   teal

Stucco

green   tan   white

Stone

grey   tan   teal

Reflections

blue   teal   white

Wrinkle

blue   tan   white

Solid colors

black   blue   light blue   light grey   tan   white

Backgrounds Selection

Page 1	Background Choice: _____	Colour: _____
Page 2	Background Choice: _____	Colour: _____
Page 3	Background Choice: _____	Colour: _____
Page 4	Background Choice: _____	Colour: _____
Page 5	Background Choice: _____	Colour: _____
Additional	Background Choice: _____	Colour: _____

Contemporary Web Site Style Sheet

Headings: **Gill Sans**

Accents: Please "x" the desired accent for your site.

Lines: ○ **Med-Thick Line**   ○ **Standard line embossed**

○ **Thin Line**   Line color utilized will be co-ordinated with background color and texture selected.

Navigational Elements:

○ **TEXT**   ○ **TEXT**

Option 1: stylized graphic featuring circular image with text   Option 2: stylized graphic featuring rectangular image with text

Backgrounds:

Concrete

blue   tan   white

Mist

blue   red   teal

Stucco

green   tan   white

Stone

grey   tan   teal

Reflections

blue   teal   white

Wrinkle

blue   tan   white

Solid colors

black   blue   light blue   light grey   tan   white

Backgrounds Selection

Page 1	Background Choice: _____	Colour: _____
Page 2	Background Choice: _____	Colour: _____
Page 3	Background Choice: _____	Colour: _____
Page 4	Background Choice: _____	Colour: _____
Page 5	Background Choice: _____	Colour: _____
Additional	Background Choice: _____	Colour: _____

Signature Web Site Style Sheet

Headings: ○ Serif   ○ San Serif

Accents: **Please "x" the desired accent for your site.**

Lines: ○ **Multi-Colour**   ○ **Standard line embossed**

○ **Twin Stripe**

○ **Metal**   **Line color utilized will be co-ordinated with background color and texture selected.**

Navigational Elements:

○ **Text** (stylized)   ○ **Text**

Option 1: this option features a text based trigger   **Option 2: features a 3D rendered button**

Backgrounds:

Concrete   **Mist**   **Stucco**

blue   tan   white   blue   red   teal   green   tan   white

Stone   **Reflections**   **Wrinkle**

grey   tan   teal   blue   teal   white   blue   tan   white

Solid colors

black   blue   light blue   light grey   tan   white

Backgrounds Selection

Page 1	Background Choice: _____	Colour: _____
Page 2	Background Choice: _____	Colour: _____
Page 3	Background Choice: _____	Colour: _____
Page 4	Background Choice: _____	Colour: _____
Page 5	Background Choice: _____	Colour: _____
Additional	Background Choice: _____	Colour: _____

c. The HQLC preview program

If you use Fleet House, your Web site will be immediately hosted on the Fleet House server so that you may see your site on the Web without delay. The address of the site will be *www.hqlc.com/yoursite*; "yoursite" will be replaced with the name you submit as your Web site address. This site will be yours to use for 60 days without obligation or payment of any setup or base service fee.

You will be allowed up to two gigabytes of traffic over the 60 days — free. If your traffic exceeds two gigabytes, Fleet House will request authorization to bill you for all additional traffic at U.S.$8/CDN$10 per gigabyte. If this request is declined, your site will be removed and no hosting charges will be incurred.

After approximately 45 days of hosting, you will receive a request for authorization for the continued provision of hosting services and an HQLC Web Site Hosting Agreement via e-mail or alternate means. You may freely choose to continue or discontinue HQLC Hosting Services.

Note: During the 60-day program period, you may remove your site immediately from the HQLC server by faxing a letter of authorization on your organization's letterhead with the signature of the primary company contact for the Web site project. This requirement is for security purposes only.

d. The HQLC server environment

Fleet House also offers an exclusive and wide range of Web site hosting services to those businesses participating in the HQLC Web site development program. You may contact Fleet House Information Management Solutions Inc. directly for information on rates.

Fleet House delivers high performance, secure Web site services on Intel-based platforms, housed in a secure computing center located in Vancouver, B.C., Canada. Web access is facilitated by a 10/25Mbs connection to the Internet.

HQLC Web site hosting services provide the continuity of service, quality, and price required to assure continued visibility on the Web for small- and medium-sized companies.

Fleet House has tremendous promotional expertise gained from working on the Internet for years and from providing promotional services to a broad client base. Fleet House can also provide promotional services for your Web site if you wish.

e. Fleet House HQLC pricing summary

1. Production Services

Creation of commercial quality Web sites from forms provided in *Winning Web Sites*.

	U.S. Dollars	Canadian Dollars
Platinum Package (5 pages of input)	$319.00	$399.00
Gold Package (3 pages of input)	$239.00	$299.00
Silver Package (2 pages of input)	$159.00	$199.00
Each additional input page (5+ total)	$60.00	$75.00

2. Hosting Services

Commercial hosting of your completed Web site on a high performance server

Shared Domain Hosting (up to 10 pages of input)	$19.95	$24.95
Full Domain Hosting (up to 10 pages of input)	$24.95	$29.95

Hosting fees include 500Mb of data traffic, additional traffic charged at $2.00 per 100Mb unit.

3. Promotional Services

Professional on-line promotion of your Web site.

Hourly	$25.00	$40.00
6 hour package	$125.00	$200.00

4. Special Services

Logo creation, animation, 3D graphics, etc. — quotes provided based on specific requirements.

Don't forget to subtract your rebate from the cost of the production service.

FLEET HOUSE ORDER FORM

Send to:
Fleet House Information Management Solutions Inc.
3849C East Hastings Street   Tel: (604) 291-1773
Burnaby, BC V5C 2H7   Fax: (604) 291-1703
Canada

❑   Yes, I would like Fleet House Information Management Solutions Inc. to create/produce my Web site. I have completed the worksheets from the Self-Counsel Press book, *Winning Web Sites* and I have enclosed them along with all graphics and text content as per the HQLC submission procedure described on page 152.

Contact name: _____

Company name: _____

Address:_____

City: _____ State/Province: _____

Zip/Postal code: _____

Telephone: (   ) _____

E-mail address: _____

Payment summary:

Web site size (input pages):   _____   Price: $ _____

British Columbia residents add 7% P.S.T. $ _____

Canadian residents add 7% G.S.T. $ _____

(If outside Canada, no taxes are payable.)

❑   I have purchased a copy of *Winning Web Sites* in the last 90 days
and wish to be credited with a rebate for its full retail purchase price.

❑   I have attached the cash register tape, or similar proof
of purchase, showing a retail price of: – ($15.95)

Total cost ❑ CDN$ ❑ US$ $ _____

Total cost to be forwarded by money order, bank draft, or certified check made payable to Fleet House Management Solutions Inc.

or,

You may charge the total cost to your MasterCard or Visa. If you choose to pay by credit card, please provide the following credit card information:

Please charge my: ❑ MasterCard   ❑ Visa

Card number:_____

Name on credit card: _____

Expiry date: _____Signature:_____

GLOSSARY

Accents

Small graphic images inserted by the production house to enhance or improve the appearance and design of the Web site. May include lines, small designs, buttons, etc.

Bandwidth

In this publication, bandwidth refers to the amount of data transfer that can be carried on a circuit or line in a given period of time. A broader or wider bandwidth can carry more information than a narrower bandwidth over the same period of time, and can therefore deliver better response times.

Browser

A browser is a tool used to read HTML documents. Common browsers include Netscape Navigator and Microsoft Explorer.

Connectivity

Refers to the software and services acquired through an Internet Service Provider for connection to the Internet.

Domain name

A domain name is the name given to a host computer on the Internet, for example, *www.yourco.com.*

E-mail

Electronic mail, or e-mail, is a system that allows people to send and receive messages via their computers. The system is usually either on a large network (the Internet), on a bulletin board (such as CompuServe), or on an office network within a company.

Extension

Extensions are suffixes added to filenames to indicate file types created by and/or used within specific application programs. A common extension is ".txt" which indicates a text-only file that may be used by a wide variety of applications.

Home page

A home page refers to the first page found at the main address of a particular Web site. The ID and Combo Pages described in this book are home pages.

Host/hosting service

A host is the server on which a Web site resides. A hosting service is usually a commercial service providing server facilities for the hosting of a Web site. A Web site may be on a dedicated server or a shared server. Depending on the client requirements, a Web site may be accessible either through a root level domain (*www.yourco.com*) or through a common domain (*www.servco.com/yourco*).

HTML

Hypertext markup language describes how document content should look on a browser. HTML codes are embedded within a document. HTML is designed to function over the World Wide Web section of the Internet and presents uniformity on a wide range of displays.

HTTP

Hypertext transport protocol (HTTP) is the underlying protocol used in the Web to support the linking of information that is fundamental to the operation of the Web facility.

Hypertext

Hypertext is a system which allows users to move between areas of a document, following a thread of related information, via textual or graphical links.

Input page

An input page is the preferred way to measure Web site content, because it is based on a tangible measurement that is recognizable to a broad range of users. Most Web site production houses measure input rather than output, because "virtual space" is not as price sensitive as physical space in a conventional hard copy medium. An input page is defined as text and graphics that can be physically contained on an 8.5" x 11" page, where the font size is 12 point and the graphics displace the text.

Interactive forms

An important feature of the Internet and the Web is the support of bidirectional communications. Customized response forms provide convenience and efficiency and often initiate customer transactions. The fast responses which interactive forms provide can accelerate the sales/promotion process.

Interactive forms require an HTML-based form, a forms-capable browser, and a script located on the server that will process and/or forward the information collected on the form to the appropriate facility or address.

Internet

The Internet is a massive, cooperative, computing network that links computer systems of all types around the globe. The Internet supports many features that can contribute to the success of any business, including e-mail and the World Wide Web, as well as Gopher, WAIS, and others. Regardless of the features used, the combination of global reach, the amazingly low cost, the support of two-way communication, and round-the-clock availability make the Internet the fastest growing tool for business today.

ISP

An Internet service provider is a commercial entity having high speed connections to the Internet. ISPs generally offer commercial shared-platform hosting services, and some provide "server parking" for those wishing to have an off-site dedicated server.

Navigational elements

Refer to the links to points within the same Web site or to points in other Web sites on the Internet. These allow you to move from point to point.

PMT

A print term which stands for "Photo Mechanical Transfer." The term PMT is usually used in the context of creating or using an original image or photo positive for camera-ready artwork. The positive image is usually supplied on a transparent sheet which is used by the printer.

Screen length

A portion of an HTML page visible within the viewing area of a browser. This usually approximates 33% to 40% of an input page.

Script

A script is a small program developed to provide services and effects within Web sites and other applications. For example, a CGI script allows you to use interactive e-mail forms that make it possible for Web surfers to send you messages from your Web site.

Server

A server is a specialized computer system composed of computing hardware (the physical server) and software (the specialized server software required to provide server functions) that provides specific services to client systems.

In this book, the servers referred to are Web servers, but there are other types of servers on the Internet, such as Gopher and WAIS. A Web server is the physical computer on which one or more Web sites are hosted. The Web server software that is running on the server facilitates the interaction between information based on the server, on other servers located on the Internet and on the client computing device that is running an HTTP-compliant browser.

URL

A URL, or uniform resource locator, is an address of an Internet site or server. A URL contains a standardized format indicating the type of program/service required to reach the information, followed by the server address and the specific file location on the server. Examples: *gopher://nstn.ns.ca* and *http://www.fleethouse.com/hqlc*.

Utility

Utilities are specialized routines or programs used to accomplish a specific function within a system. They are usually associated with repetitive functions. For example, a search function is a utility.

Web page

A Web page is any HTML page that can be displayed on a screen by a browser.

Web site

A Web site is a collection of HTML pages hosted on a Web server accessible at an URL and usually featuring one or more related information segments. Commercial Web sites may be used for promotion, facilitating business transactions, gathering timely information, and extending customer support services.

WWW

The World Wide Web is a hypertext-based, distributed information system spanning an enormous combination of interlinked computer systems. The World Wide Web facility, or Web, supports the rapid movement of information between computers located anywhere around the globe. The broad reach, relative low cost, and ability to handle text, sound, graphics, and images makes this a favored medium for business.